Understanding E-Minis:
Trading to Win

Traders Press, Inc.®
PO Box 6206
Greenville, SC 29606

Serving Traders since 1975

Jerry Williams, M.D.

ISBN: 0-934380-90-2
Published by **Traders Press, Inc.**®

Editing by: *Roger Reimer*
&
Teresa Darty Alligood
Layout and Cover Design by: *Teresa Darty Alligood*

Traders Press, Inc.®
PO Box 6206
Greenville, SC 29606

Serving Traders since 1975

800-927-8222 / 864-298-0222 Fax 864-298-0221
catalog@traderspress.com
http://www.traderspress.com

DEDICATION

This book is dedicated to my parents, my wife, our two beautiful daughters Lauren and Nicole, and my trading partner, Kevin. My Mom and Dad taught me the principle that exists in the futures markets. There can only be losers or winners in life. They taught me the sheer will to survive against all odds and to accept responsibility for my mistakes. My wonderful wife and daughters have always given me strength and encouragement to believe in myself. Kevin has become my friend and trading partner. He has taught me the importance of changing with the markets and never being satisfied with today, but becoming a better trader tomorrow.

ACKNOWLEDGEMENTS

Special thanks to Cindy Chiodo who worked hard to organize our manuscript.

Special thanks to E-Signal for permission to reprint charts from their graphics and software program.

Publisher's Foreword

When I first became involved in futures trading some 40 years ago, the most active markets were the grains, pork bellies, and other agricultural markets. As the decades have passed, the most active futures markets have changed from tangible, marketable goods, to intangibles such as Eurodollars, T-bonds, and the like. With the advent of the "E-mini" contracts in various markets, but primarily in the stock indices came a virtual explosion of trading interest. Today, the E-mini futures, especially in the S&P and the NASDAQ (often alluded to as the "Spoo" and the "Naz") are far and away the biggest trading game in town.

Many individuals who had never been involved in futures trading before were attracted by the tremendous popularity and liquidity of these trading vehicles and became active participants in the "game". Unfortunately, many if not most of them were unfamiliar with many of the ideas and concepts which might make the difference between their trading profitably or unprofitably. There has been a dire need for a comprehensive source which addresses the learning needs of these new traders. It is our hope that the ideas, tips, and techniques taught in this book will prove helpful to the many new traders in this fascinating arena.

Traders Press has as its primary goal the publication and distribution of high quality materials related to trading, which will enable traders to become more self-sufficient, better educated, and hopefully more profitable traders. Our other products may be viewed, and our catalog ordered on **http://www.traderspress.com.** Be sure to visit us there.

Edward D. Dobson

Edward D. Dobson, President   **January 11, 2004**
Traders Press, Inc.®

TABLE OF CONTENTS

Introduction	1
What Markets to Trade	3
Why is Leverage the Key Factor?	5
Characteristics of E-Mini Contracts	6
What is a Stock	7
Contract Months	9
Are There Secrets to Trading the E-Minis?	10
Do You Use Fundamental or Technical Analysis?	11
Slippage and Commissions	12
What Do I Need to Trade the E-Minis?	13
Is There Really a High Probability Trading System?	16
Basic Price Chart Configurations / Types of Charts	17
Charts and Time Frames	23
Support and Resistance	28
Pivot Points	29
High-Low-Close-Open Relationship	31
Normal Trading Day	32
Volume	35
Single Bar Patterns	37
Breakout Trades	38
Reversal Trades – Bar Charts	41
Major Bearish Reversal Signals – Candlestick Charts	47
Other Reversal Signals – Candlestick Charts	54
Summary of Candlesticks	63
Candlestick Summary	64
Time and Sales	65
Market Breadth Indicators	66
Market Trading Indicators	86
Miscellaneous Indicators	113
Commitment of Traders Report	114
Fair Value and Program Trading	115
Summary of Market Indicators	116
Economic Numbers	118
The Greenspan Effect	121
Prepare for the Trading Day	123
Risk Management	126
The Critical Importance of Orders	130
Trading Strategies	132
Closing Statement	196
Bibliography	197

THE ESSENTIALS OF EFFECTIVE E-MINI TRADING

INTRODUCTION

The personal computer age and the 'information superhighway' have allowed off-floor day traders to compete with the floor traders at the futures exchanges. In the past, floor traders have dominated off-floor investors by paying lower commissions, having immediate access to price information, and being able to sense the changing mood of the trading pits. Today, this advantage is diminishing as the result of on-line discount brokers and the ability to send orders directly to the floor in many futures markets. The playing field is also being leveled with the introduction of E-MINI contracts in the S&P 500 and NASDAQ-100 indices. Their introduction has resulted in tremendous liquidity and volatility (movement) in these markets. A trader needs liquidity to enter and exit positions with ease and volatility to guarantee that the trading vehicle he chooses will move enough to make money.

Unfortunately, most individuals who trade futures will lose money. Professionals who have been successful in other businesses often begin trading futures thinking that it is an easy way to make money. Soon, they watch their trading accounts dwindle to nothing. The excitement and bright lights of trading often overshadow the possibility of downside risk. For every winner in the futures market, there has to be a loser. This is unlike rising prices in the stock market, where many individuals can become richer with higher stock prices. If there are so many losers, why risk hard earned capital on such a small chance of success? It is known that traders who follow a trading plan, control risk, understand leverage and control their emotions can beat the odds.

This book is for the trader who wants to start with a better understanding of the markets and learn how to profit from short-term price fluctuations in a bull or bear market. Do not be lured into the idea that it is easy for beginners to make money. There is no such thing as a free lunch on Wall Street. The markets give a final verdict of the market's value every trading day at the close. It is important to realize that this verdict will not be favorable if you enter the trading battle unprepared. Traders need to realize that skill and success in the markets is not inherited, but acquired through hard work, education, patience, and emotional discipline. We hope this book will help you to become a better trader and not a gambler (Figure 1).

TRADERS	GAMBLERS

IN THE MARKETS, WE HAVE THE OPTION OF BECOMING A TRADER OR A GAMBLER. A TRADER IS SOMEONE WHO STUDIES THE MARKETS, HAS AN ORGANIZED TRADING PLAN, KEEPS LOSSES TO A MINIMUM, AND USES GOOD LOGIC IN TRADING. A GAMBLER IS SOMEONE WHO USES EMOTION TO MAKE TRADING DECISIONS AND WALKS INTO THE TRADING BATTLE WITHOUT A PLAN. HE WILL USUALLY LET FEAR AND GREED CONTROL HIS TRADING DESTINY.

Figure 1

WHAT MARKETS TO TRADE ?

We were drawn to the E-Mini contracts of the S&P 500 and NASDAQ due to the ease of getting into and out of trades with minimal slippage. At this time, we do not trade the other E-Mini contracts for the Dow, Russell 2000, crude oil, Midcap 400 or natural gas because of lower liquidity. E-Mini contracts are attractive to beginning traders because of their lower initial margin requirements. These markets offer several advantages that work in favor for the day trader, including:

- **LIQUIDITY**

  The market for the S&P 500 and NASDAQ-100 have such a high trading volume that it is easy to get in or out of a trade.

- **VOLATILITY**

  The S&P 500 and NASDAQ Indices have good price volatility with upward and downward price movements in short time periods that can create good trading opportunities.

- **LEVERAGE**

  Leverage gives a trader a chance to make a large return on his money with a small investment. A trader may trade one E-Mini contract with an account of less than $5,000 even though the value of the contract may be worth more than $50,000.

- ## RISK CONTROL

  It is easy to place stop loss orders to decrease losses and preserve trading capital when establishing a trading position.

- ## ACCESSIBILITY

  The doors never close and trading can be accomplished nearly 24 hours a day.

WHY IS LEVERAGE THE KEY FACTOR FOR PROFITS AND LOSSES IN TRADING THE E-MINIS?

LEVERAGE IS LIKE A DOUBLE-EDGED SWORD THAT CAN LEAD TO PROFITS OR LOSSES.

A trader needs to put up a small percentage of the futures contract value in order to trade the E-Mini futures. If the price of the S&P E-Mini is 900, then the total cost of the contract is $45,000. The margin requirement to trade one E-Mini contract is usually less than $5,000. This means that for less than $5000, a trader can trade or control one contract, which is worth $45,000. This is unlike a stock trader who would have to put up $25,000 of margin to buy $50,000 worth of stock.

For Example:

If you only had to put up 10% of a contract's value, your gains or losses will occur at 10 times the change in price. If your E-Mini contract value goes up 10%, your gain will be 100%. If the futures contract value goes down 5%, you will lose 50%. This is an illustration of how futures trading has unlimited rewards and risks.

CHARACTERISTICS OF 2 BEST E-MINI CONTRACTS

E-MINI S&P 500

- Ticker Symbol - ES
- Exchange - Chicago Mercantile Exchange
- Value of 1 Tick - 0.25 = $12.50
- Contract Value - $50 * S&P price ( ) = Contract Value
- Trading Hours - 5:30 pm Sunday to 3:15 pm Friday (Central Time)
- Contract Months - March, June, September, and December.
- Last Trading Day - Up to 8:30 a.m. on 3rd Friday of contract month.
- Final Settlement
  Date - The 3rd Friday of contract month.

E-MNI NASDAQ-100

- Ticker Symbol - NQ
- Exchange - Chicago Mercantile Exchange
- Value of 1 Tick - 0.50 = $10.00
- Contract Value - $20 * NASDAQ price ( ) = Contract Value
- Trading Hours - 5:30 pm Sunday to 3:15 pm Friday (Central Time)
- Contract Months - March, June, September, and December.
- Last Trading Day - Up to 8:30 a.m. on 3rd Friday of contract month.
- Final Settlement
  Date - The 3rd Friday of contract month.

The E-Mini futures contracts have attracted numerous small investors since they are traded exclusively in an electronic marketplace. The full size S&P futures contract is traded on the exchange floor by brokers and traders using the "open outcry" auction method. This is typically less efficient and allows more slippage for the small investor who is unable to trade the full size S&P futures contract without assuming a higher level of risk. The benefit that the E-Mini provides to traders is a chance to trade with less margin than stocks and no restriction on short selling. Short selling futures does not require an up tick.

WHAT IS A STOCK INDEX?

A stock index represents a portfolio of stocks grouped in a certain way. A particular index can provide a quick picture of how a specific group of stocks is performing when compared to another group of stocks (i.e., the S&P 500 Index versus the Russell 2000 Index). Trading stock indices is easier than trying to pick an individual winning stock. Through the use of stock indices, an investor can gain exposure to a certain segment of the market such as a technology, blue-chip, or mid-cap. Another approach to using stock indices is to purchase a broad based index that can represent the entire stock market.

Index futures closely follow the price movement of their respective underlying cash index. The stock index futures are traded in terms of the number of contracts. Each contract is to buy or sell a fixed value of the index. The value of the index is obtained by multiplying the price of the index times the contract multiplier. Most indices are capitalization weighted, which means that the stocks with the most shares are weighted the heaviest in the index and thus have the most influence on movement. This is unlike the price-weighted index such as the Dow-Jones Industrial Index where the stocks with the highest price carry the most influence.

INDEX FUTURES CONTRACT MULTIPLIERS

- S&P 500   - $250
- E-Mini 500   - $50
- NASDAQ 100   - $100
- E-Mini NASDAQ - $20

When you multiply the contract multiplier times the price of the E-Mini contract, the result is the full value of one contract.

Example—If the price of the S&P is 900
*A.   E-Mini S&P ($50 * 900) = $45,000, which is value of 1 contract.*

S&P 500 INDEX

- Benchmark used by professionals to measure portfolio performance
- Based upon stock prices of 500 large capitalization companies
- Market value is equal to 80% of the value of all stocks on exchange
- Includes companies such as Microsoft, General Electric, and General Motors

S&P MIDCAP 400 INDEX

- Tracks performance of medium capitalization companies rather than large-cap companies
- Includes companies such as Barnes and Nobles

RUSSELL 2000 INDEX

- Based upon 2000 stocks that are small capitalization

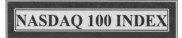

NASDAQ 100 INDEX

- Based upon 100 companies
- Capitalization weighted• Includes companies such as Microsoft, Intel, and Cisco

The S&P 500, MIDCAP 400, and RUSSELL 2000 represent close to 94% of the TOTAL U.S. MARKET VALUE. The Top 40 S&P 500 stocks account for about 50% of the market capitalization of the S&P 500 index.

CONTRACT MONTHS

Most indices settle on a quarterly cycle that includes the months of March, June, September, and December. The contract month identifies the month in which the futures contract terminates. This is also called the "delivery month" and helps to ensure that the futures price converges with the cash market price of the index. Most traders establish a new position prior to contract expiration.

CONTRACT MONTH SYMBOLS

March	-	H
June	-	M
September	-	U
December	-	Z

WHAT IS A TICK?

- A Tick is the minimum price movement of an index future
- Tick value = minimum tick size times the contract multiplier

E-Mini NASDAQ – $0.5 * 20 = \$10$

E-Mini S&P   – $0.25 * 50 = \$12.50$

ARE THERE SECRETS TO TRADING THE E-MINIS?

There are no secrets to trading the stock index futures. A lot of traders are taught to buy low and sell high. It all sounds so easy to a new investor. The thought of making a lot of money very quickly overpowers the reality of trading. We have all been taught from a historical perspective that the stock market usually goes up over time. This generalization can be deadly when you're trading and find out the hard way that the stock market can go down a lot faster than it goes up.

We all witnessed the NASDAQ meltdown that started in March of 2000 when many technology companies literally went up in smoke. Many 'investors' bought companies like Yahoo at $200 per share only to watch them fall to less than $20 per share. This taught us the lesson that a 'buy and hold' strategy of investing can be dangerous in a volatile market.

DO YOU USE FUNDAMENTAL OR TECHNICAL ANALYSIS?

Trying to determine whether to use fundamental analysis or technical analysis is like the battle between the different political parties, where each one feels that their method is the 'holy grail.' Fundamental analysis relies on extensive review of earnings and Price/Earnings ratios to see if a company's financial status is promising. Investors who use fundamental analysis do not worry about daily whipsaws in the market, but are looking for steady investments that will grow in value over time. This analysis requires hours of research that can become all consuming for an individual investor.

Many traders have turned to technical analysis because they believe that prices move in repeating and identifiable patterns. Traders who use technical analysis point to three basic principles that support this idea:

PRICE IS KING AND EVERYTHING IS ALREADY DISCOUNTED

PRICES MOVE IN TRENDS

MARKET ACTION REPEATS ITSELF OVER AND OVER AGAIN

The most important principle is that 'Price is King' and all knowledge (economic, political, or psychological) is already reflected in prices. Changes in supply and demand are reflected in the price. This is evidenced by professional traders who say to "sell on good news" because the good news is already reflected in the price. How many times have you seen good news about a stock on CNBC result in a decline in the stock's price over the next few months? What about a high flying stock that makes the cover of Business Week? *Usually, by the time a stock makes the front cover of a major news magazine, everyone has already bought the stock and it cannot go much higher because all of the strong buying has already occurred.*

The second principle is that prices move in trends, which can persist until the price movement slows and finally reverses direction. A smart trader knows that following the trend increases their chance of making money.

The final principle is that market action will repeat itself over and over again. A certain price pattern may be repeated on a chart and may cause traders to act in the same as they have in the past. Human beings are creatures of habit and usually react in the same way, which creates footprints in the price pattern that can be easily followed.

Technical analysis works because many professional traders predict how other investors will react based upon certain technical analysis patterns and indicators. They tend to trade opposite the amateurs and enter when the trade starts to reverse which usually results in a greater chance of profits. Technical analysis allows them to enter a trade with minimal risk.

SLIPPAGE AND COMMISSIONS – THE HIDDEN ENEMY

The markets are set up for the trader to lose money with slippage and commissions. Most amateur traders are surprised to learn that the odds are stacked against them to win. A trader must pay commissions for entering and exiting a "round turn" trade that is payable when you exit the trade. This cost can vary from less than $5 to more than $30 for full service brokers. Slippage is the term used to define the difference between your order price and the price at which it gets filled.

For example, when a trader enters a 'market order,' it is seldom filled at the best price. Using a 'market order' is a good way to increase your odds of losing; whereas a 'limit order' is filled at your price or not at all. The markets are like casinos in that they need a fresh supply of losers to support the exchanges, regulators and brokers. A trader has to deal with commissions and slippage, which will always be an important barrier to success and is illustrated below:

1. Buy 1 S&P E-Mini contracts at 900
    Sell 1 S&P E-Mini contracts at 902
    900 – 902 = 2 points profits (1 point = $50)
    Commission costs = $25 per round turn
    Profit($100) minus Commission ($25) = $75
    Commission costs are 25% of the trade

2. Enter market order to buy 1 S&P E-Mini contracts at 900
    Filled at 900.25
    Difference between 900 and 900.25 = .25 (slippage)
    .25 = $12.75
    Total slippage is $12.75 for 1 contract

SLIPPAGE ($12.75) plus COMMISSION ($25) = $37.75

$100 - $37.75 = $62.25 profits

THE COST FOR SLIPPAGE AND COMMISSION WAS 38% OF TRADE

This illustration shows how commissions and slippage can affect profits on the bottom line. If a limit order had been used in the above scenario to enter the trade at 900 rather than 900.25, $12.75 would have been saved. That is 13% of our trade gross profit lost for slippage. A trader needs to realize that commission and slippage must be overcome before any profits are taken home.

WHAT DO I NEED TO TRADE THE E-MINI FUTURES

RELIABLE BROKER

Trading the E-Mini futures without a good broker is like trying to skip across alligators in the water and hoping you make it to the shore. We all have heard of nightmare stories where a trader was unable to get out of a losing position and lost hundreds to thousands of dollars. Before putting your hard earned money in a broker's hand, make sure their system platform is dependable and does not go down on a frequent basis. Also, investigate to see if they have a backup computer system as a safeguard in the event of a server problem.

In order to trade the E-Mini contracts, a broker must have good execution speed. A day trader must be able to get the best price possible to become profitable in the long run. Bad fills and slippage are a death sentence for a futures trader over time. Trade confirmation must be rapid and not affected by high trading volumes.

E-Mini quotes must be reliable and reproducible. If a trader gets a bad quote, which can occur due to server or Internet problems, it could turn into a tremendous loss. Many good traders rely on two different quote services to confirm their trades.

Commission costs can end your trading career early. An amateur trader may think commission costs are negligible, but over time commissions can turn into a lot of money. A day trader who does a lot of scalp trades during the day can have a high percentage of profits taken away because of high commission costs.

The quality of phone service access is critical regarding order executions and confirmations. What if you want to place an entry order or exit a trade and no one answers the telephone? What do you do if you are put on hold while the losses continue to increase? A trader needs a broker that has reasonable response times on the telephone.

A GOOD COMPUTER SYSTEM

A trader needs a reliable computer with at least a Pentium 3 or 4 microprocessor and a minimum of 256 megabyte RAM (random access memory). Do not think that you can take an old computer with an outdated operating system and compete in the fast moving futures markets. If you try to cut corners on costs with your computer system, it will cost you money in the long run.

Most traders use two monitors because of the difficulty in putting all of the real time information onto one screen. The second monitor can be easily installed with a video card. 19" monitors are much easier on the eyes than 15" and 17" monitors.

The computer operating system needs to be Windows 2000 or Windows XP. These operating systems are less likely to freeze up during a trade and allow a winning trade to turn into a losing one. *Avoid using Linux operating systems since most of the trading software is written for the Windows platform.*

RELIABLE INTERNET CONNECTION

The trading game requires high performance and a rapid Internet connection. Dial up connections can be slow and unreliable. Cable or DSL Internet service is the best for day trading. These services are decreasing in price as more providers are entering the market and making it more competitive.

REAL TIME DATA

Trading the E-Minis requires tick-by-tick data for input in making trading decisions. There are numerous data vendors that can provide real-time and delayed data. Make sure that your trading software properly interacts with the data vendor's signal and that the transmission time to your screen is as short as possible. Talk to other traders and get recommendations for vendors that are reliable and cost effective.

CAPITAL

The money that you use for day trading should be money that you can afford to lose. Do not use money that has been set back for retirement, the children's education or emergencies to trade the E-Mini futures. You cannot trade effectively if you are using money that will be needed for bills or daily necessities. Trading requires self-discipline and control that can be greatly influenced by the current balance of your bank account. The starting amount of capital needs to be an amount that you feel comfortable with and meets the financial requirements of your broker. In the event of a losing streak, there is a greater risk to traders who have smaller accounts. With an account of less than $5,000, you should only trade one contract. If you are charged $25 for a round turn to trade E-Minis you will need a move of 0.5 index points to breakeven. This means that your profit for a one point move in the S&P is only $25 (normal profit is $50 for one point move), which is a commission rate of 50%. This illustrates the power of commissions in decreasing the number of winning traders. These commissions can be offset by finding a discount broker with lower costs and good service.

IS THERE REALLY A HIGH PROBABILITY TRADING SYSTEM?

A new trader will be bombarded by vendors who claim to have a high probability trading system that can beat the markets. The words 'high probability' assumes a high success rate. Many vendors make unrealistic claims about their system's performance in order to convince new traders that they can steal money from the markets. The term "high probability" has been coined by the trading industry. The truth is that most professional traders are considered good if they have a 50% to 60% winning average.

A doctor telling his patients that his operation success rate was 60% would have a large stampede for the door in elective surgeries. Trading cannot be compared to a doctor's success rate, but a trader can be successful with 50% winners by understanding statistical probability. Normal trade distribution takes the form of the classic "bell shaped standard deviation curve." Most of our trading will show up as small winners or losers in the middle range of the curve with the ends of the bell shaped curve showing the big winners and/or losers, which compose a smaller proportion of our trade results.

This concept of statistical probability emphasizes that with 50 percent winners versus losers and the same trade average, would yield a breakeven month. If we cut our losses immediately and let our winners run, we can show profitable trading results. Trading is like a baseball player who is not able to hit a home run every time he bats. He also has singles and strikeouts. Babe Ruth had a lot of strikeouts, but he will always be remembered as the "Homerun King." This concept illustrates that it takes more than a good system to be a successful trader. A trader has to know when to cut his losses and get out of a trade. The power of fear and greed will make a trader watch a small loss turn into catastrophic lost.

Many salesmen of these so-called "high probability" trading systems don't even trade their systems. These vendors need to post an actual report card of their trades that were filled by a brokerage firm. This report would show actual entries and exits with true profits and losses. A trader could get a true picture of the trading system from this report. What usually happens at trade shows is that a trader is only shown examples of the "big winners." The hype and emotion are emphasized with little emphasis on potential downside risk. A successful trader must have a good trading system and understand how to manage trades using the concepts of probability.

BASIC PRICE CHART CONFIGURATION

FOUR TYPES OF PRICE CHARTS

- Bar Chart
- Line Chart
- Point and Figure Chart
- Japanese Candlestick Chart

Prices represent the daily tug-of-war between the bears and bulls. Small price bars represent a small battle; while large bars represent an all out war with fighting all over the screen. If we close higher for the day, the bulls have kicked the bears back to their caves. If we close lower for the time period, the bears have made the bulls tuck their tails and run for cover (Figure 1).

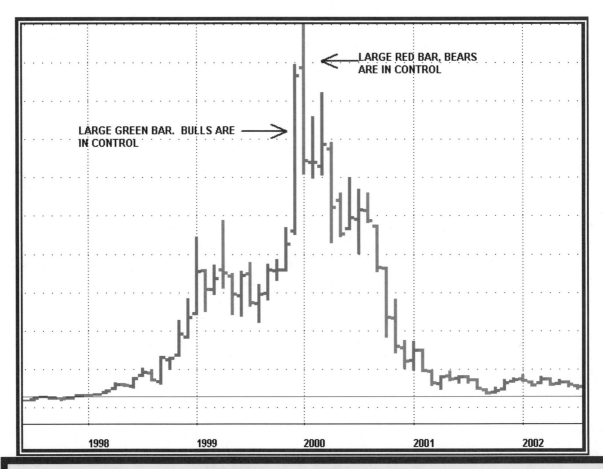

MONTHLY CHART OF YAHOO

This chart shows the rise and fall of Yahoo. The large green bar in the uptrend shows the bulls in control. This large green bar suggests more buyers than sellers. The stock hit a top and was followed by a large red bar. This suggests the bulls were losing the battle and tucked their tails and ran for cover. There is now more selling than buying. Yahoo fell from over $200 per share to less than $20 per share.

Figure 1

BAR CHARTS

- Vertical line　　　-　　　High and Low of time period

- Closing price　　-　　　Small protrusion to the right is controlled by professional buying or selling.

　　　　　　　　　　　　If markets closed higher - Professionals buying
　　　　　　　　　　　　If markets closed lower - Professionals selling

- Opening price　-　　Small protrusion to the left is due to amateur buying or selling before the market opens. Usually occur near high or low of day.

- Small or Normal Size Bar　　　Good to enter market. There is less slippage and volatility.

- Large Bar　　-　　Good for taking profits. Hard to enter market due to high volatility and rapid movement. Do not use a market order to enter on a large bar.

LINE CHARTS

- Plots only closing prices in a line (Figure 2B).

POINT AND FIGURE CHARTS

1. They have been around longer than bar charts.
2. Previously used by professional traders in the pits.
3. The charts are based on price only and there is no reference to volume or time on the chart (Figure 2A).
4. Some traders feel they are helpful to find support and resistance and point out possible overbought and oversold areas.

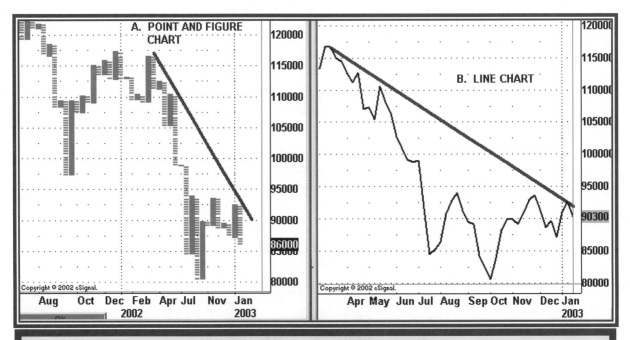

WEEKLY CHARTS OF S&P FUTURES
BOTH CHARTS SHOW DOWNTREND

CHART A   Point-and-figure chart. Point-and-figure charts were first used by floor traders. Good for locating support and resistance areas.

CHART B   Line chart of closing prices.

Figure 2A, 2B

JAPANESE CANDLESTICK CHARTS

- Called Candlestick charts because lines look like candles and wicks
- Tip of candle represents high and low called shadows (wicks)
- Body represents opening and closing prices (Figure 3)
- Body is red when closing price is less than the opening price
- Body is green when closing price is greater than the opening price
- Long green body means the bulls are in control
- Long red body means the bears are in control
- A small body (green or red) means the bull and bears are equal in strength and the trend may change
- Candle charting tools are mainly reversal tools and are most effective when the market is overbought or oversold
- See (Figure 4), which compares bar charts with candlestick charts

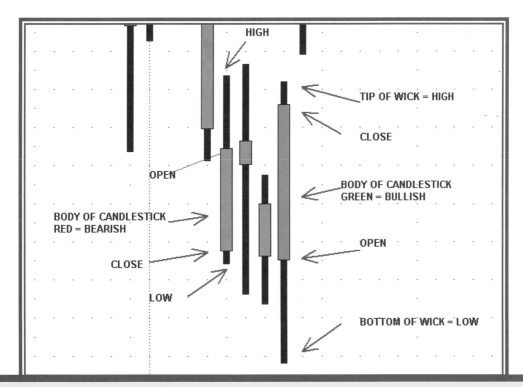

JAPANESE CANDLESTICK CHARTS

They derive their names because the lines look like candles and wicks. Wicks at each end represent the high and low. The body shows the open and close. When the candle is green the closing price is greater than the opening price. When the candle is red the closing price is less than the opening price.

Figure 3

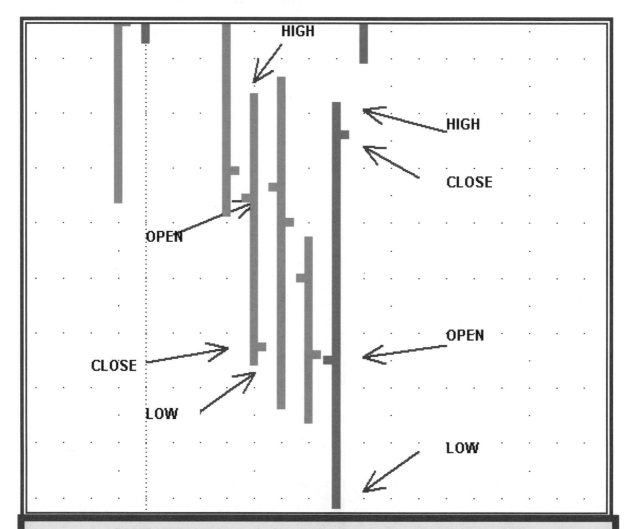

COMPARISION OF BAR CHARTS AND CANDLESTICK CHARTS

Bar charts do not emphasize the body like the Japanese candlesticks. The Japanese feel that the opening and closing prices are the essence of price movement. Candlestick charts may be better predictors of price reversals when compared to bar charts.

Figure 4

CHARTS AND TIME FRAMES

Charts can be used to look at different time frames of an individual stock, stock index or futures contract to help determine the overall trend of the market. This can be confusing to a trader when it seems that the market is moving in two different directions at the same time. While the 30-minute chart on the E-Mini contract may show an uptrend, the 5-minute chart may show a downtrend. This is an example of why a trader cannot develop tunnel vision and look only in one direction. A smart trader uses the longer time frame to decide whether to go short or long and the shorter time frame to enter and exit the trade. If the 30-minute chart is showing a downtrend, short the market at the top of up waves on the 5-minute chart. If the 30-minute chart is showing an uptrend, buy at the bottoms of down waves on the 5-minute chart.

Prices move into uptrends and follow into downtrends and seem to travel on invisible highways on the trading screen. Trendlines can be used to illustrate the trend and show when it is changing direction. A rising trendline leads to higher highs and shows that the bulls are in control while a declining trendline leads to lower lows and shows that the bears are in control. When the angle of a rising or declining trendline is greater than 60 degrees, strong reversals can result. These strong reversals at tops of rallies or bottoms of declines are evident when a spike is formed. The spike tells the trader that the market is rejecting that price and that the market is ripe for a reversal and a move the opposite direction. Trader Vic reported a simple method for drawing trendlines that is outlined below:

FOR UPTRENDS

A.   Draw a trendline from lowest low to the lowest low preceding the highest high (Figure 5A).

B.   The trendline cannot pass through prices between the two points.

HIGH

LOW

5 12 20 26 2 9 17 23 2 9 16 23 30 6 13 20 27 4
1998   Feb   Mar   Apr   May

TRENDLINE FOR UPTREND – S&P 500 FUTURES

Find the current high and look to the left to find the most recent swing low. Then look to the left to find the lowest swing low. If a trendline does not pass through any candles between the two swing lows, it is a valid trendline.

Figure 5A

FOR DOWNTRENDS

A.   Draw a trendline from highest high to the highest high preceding the lowest low (Figure 5B).

B.   The trendline cannot pass through prices between the two points.

LOW

S&P E-MINI FUTURES DAILY CHART – DOWNTREND
Find the lowest low and look to the left to find the higher swing high. Then look to the left to find the highest swing high and then draw a trendline connecting the highest swing high to the lower swing high. If this trendline does not pass through any candles, it is valid.

Figure 5B

This approach can be used to identify a trend change and is called the 3 B's for a trend change.

3 B's For A Long Trade

1. Broken trendline (Figure 6A)
2. Back test of previous low
3. Breakout above resistance or high

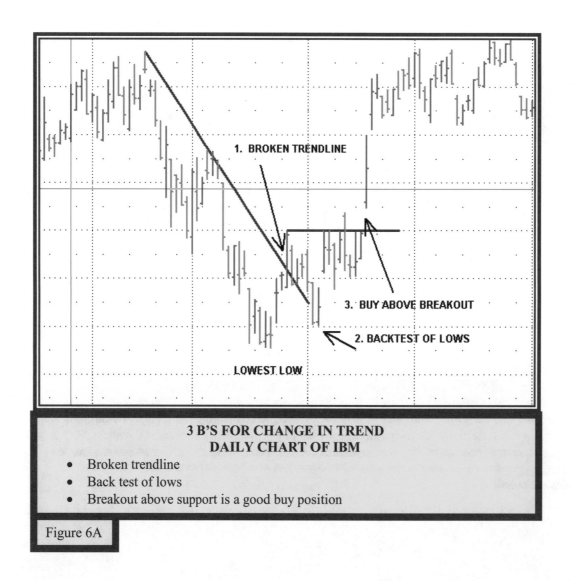

3 B'S FOR CHANGE IN TREND
DAILY CHART OF IBM

- Broken trendline
- Back test of lows
- Breakout above support is a good buy position

Figure 6A

3 B's For Short Trade

- Broken trendline (Figure 6B)
- Back test of previous high
- Breakout below support or low

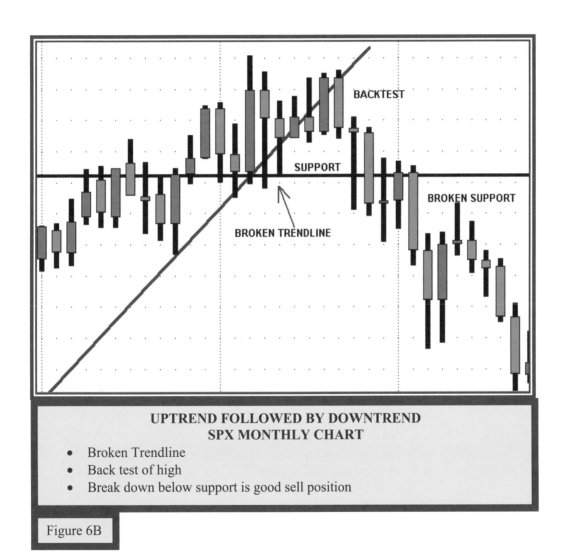

UPTREND FOLLOWED BY DOWNTREND
SPX MONTHLY CHART

- Broken Trendline
- Back test of high
- Break down below support is good sell position

Figure 6B

SUPPORT AND RESISTANCE - PRICES ARE TRAPPED IN BETWEEN

SUPPORT

- Floor below the prices
- Prices tend to bounce off of support
- Enough buyers prevent decline of stock prices through support

RESISTANCE

- Ceiling above the prices
- Prices tend to bounce away from resistance
- Enough sellers stop rise of stock price through resistance

Prices act like a ping-pong ball that bounces between support and resistance (Figure 7). Sellers drive prices down like the ball back to support and buyers push the ball up back to resistance. Prices seem to be sandwiched between support and resistance until a breakout of the range occurs. A true breakout is more likely to occur with increased volume.

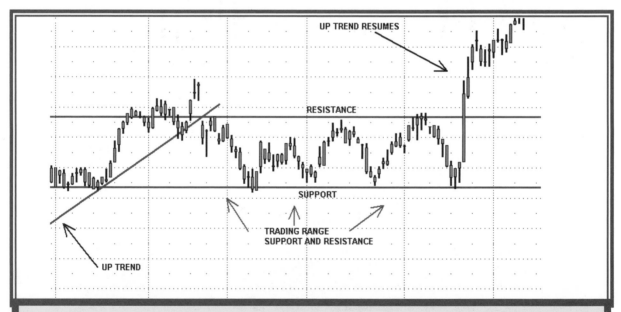

SUPPORT AND RESISTENCE DAILY CHART OF IBM
- IBM shows an uptrend followed by area of consolidation (trading range), before resuming its original upward direction.
- The trading range shows support (floor) and resistance (ceiling) where prices bounce back and forth like a ping- pong ball between support and resistance.

Figure 7

PIVOT POINTS

Futures markets create an equilibrium (pivot point) around which trading activity occurs. Floor traders use this point to adjust their bids and offers. Here is this simple formula that is used by floor traders.

H = Previous day's high
L = Previous day's low
C = Previous day's close

Pivot Point = (H + L + C) divided by 3
First Resistance Level = (2 * Pivot) - L
First Support Level = (2 * Pivot) - H
Second Resistance Level = Pivot + (First Resistance - First Support)
Second Support Level = Pivot - (First Resistance - First Support)

- Pivot points are most useful when floor traders are in control and there is no outstanding news to move the market.

- Floor traders tend to move the market between the pivot point and first level of support and resistance.

- If price moves through the pivot point on increased volume, the trend will likely continue. If price hits the pivot and is unable to continue, the trend will probably reverse.

- If the first support and resistance are penetrated, this usually results in a flurry of breakout trades in the direction of the trend from other traders off of the floor.

- When the price activity reaches first resistance or support, look at other indicators to see if you are bullish or bearish on the market. This will help to tell you if the trend is about to reverse or continue.

- If prices break above the pivot point, it is considered a bullish signal. If prices break below the pivot point, it is considered a bearish signal. The first support level is a good place to take profits, if you go short below the open. Usually, the second support level is the expected low of the day. The exception is when you have strong news that can move the market through the first and second support level. It is better to not go long unless the prices are above the pivot. The profit target for a long trade would be the first and second resistance levels.

- Gopalakrishnan reported in *Technical Analysis of Stocks and Commodities Magazine* that it is important to determine the overall trend of the pivot. This is done by comparing the three-day and five-day moving average of the pivot point with today's pivot. If today's pivot point is greater than the averages, it indicates a bullish market. If the pivot is less than the averages, a bearish market is indicated. This article emphasizes the importance of not trading against the trend.

HIGH - LOW - CLOSE - RELATIONSHIP

- There is a strong relationship between the high, low and closing prices of the day.

- A market that closes near its daily high is bullish. The buyers have overpowered the sellers.

- A market that closes near its low is bearish. The sellers have overpowered the buyers.

OPEN - CLOSE RELATIONSHIP

- A market that closes higher than it opens suggests increased buying.

- A market that closes lower than its open suggests increased selling.

- A market that closes higher than the open and near its high is very bullish.

- A market that closes lower than its open and near its low is very bearish.

NORMAL TRADING DAY

- The distribution of trades looks like a parabolic or bell shaped curve.

- The majority of trading occurs in the middle of the curve or range (Figure 8).

- The trading time that is spent at the highs and lows of the day is typically only a few minutes out of the entire trading day.

- Professionals love to buy the low of the day and sell the high of the day.   This pushes prices back toward the middle of the curve (Figure 9).

- In the majority of the trading days, the trend is back to the middle of the curve where supply and demand is in equilibrium.

- Normally, markets do not run because prices are pushed back toward equilibrium. When we do see a big up or down day, it is because the tug-of-war between the bulls and bears has been broken.   This creates disequilibrium, which is the exception, rather than the rule.

- In order to diagnose a state of disequilibrium, which could lead to a big breakout day, we have to observe how prices behave at new lows and new highs.

- If prices are rejected at a new high or new low, it is a good sign that the market is reversing direction. A breakout trade that does not materialize, needs to be exited immediately. Taking a position for a move in the opposite direction is a good strategy for a failed breakout trade.

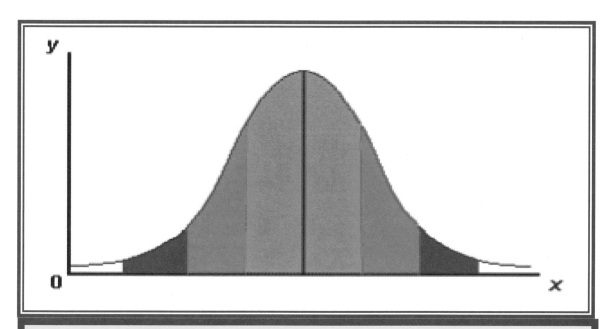

STANDARD DEVIATION BELL SHAPED CURVE

The three colors illustrate the standard deviation units of the bell shaped curve. The first standard deviation (red color), second standard deviation (green color), and third standard deviation (blue color). The majority of the time, the market will stay in the first standard deviation with some movement into the second standard deviation. The highs and lows of a trading day only last a few minutes out of the trading day and are represented in the blue colors which is the third standard deviation.

Figure 8

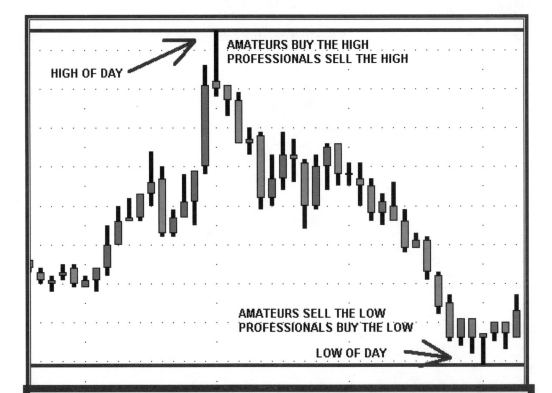

PROFESSIONAL VERSES AMATEUR TRADING STYLES – S&P FUTURES

- Professional traders act like bulldozers and push prices to the middle of the trading range by selling the highs and buying the lows. They are usually right the majority of the time since the market only breaks out of a trading range 30% of the time.
- Amateurs try to take out the highs and lows. This works well in a strong bull or bear market when the market is trending strong in one direction. In today's markets the high and low breakouts are few and far between.

Figure 9

- Volume is the engine that pulls the E-Mini train and is viewed as a measure of market strength or weakness.

- Volume measures the number of contracts of the E-Mini that have changed hands during a specific time period.

- If volume is increasing, the engine is pulling stronger and the price trend will continue.

- If volume is decreasing the engine is running out of steam and the price trend will consolidate or reverse.

- Volume will vary during the trading day and will be greatest the open and   close. Volume decreases during lunchtime (Figure 10).

PRICE	VOLUME	RESULT
Rising	Up	Bullish
Rising	Down	Bearish
Decreasing	Up	Bearish
Decreasing	Down	Bullish

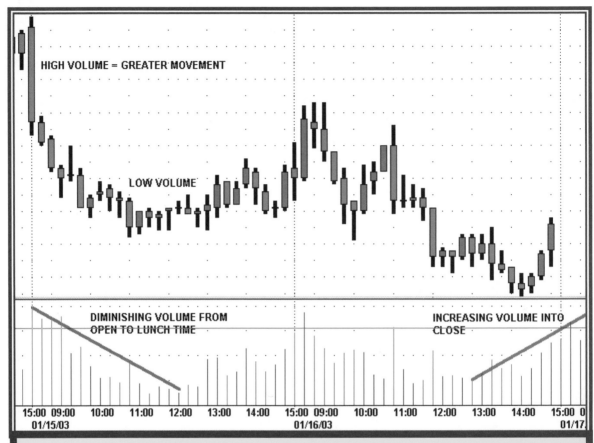

HIGH VOLUME = GREATER MOVEMENT

LOW VOLUME

DIMINISHING VOLUME FROM
OPEN TO LUNCH TIME

INCREASING VOLUME INTO
CLOSE

15:00 09:00   10:00   11:00   12:00   13:00   14:00   15:00 09:00   10:00   11:00   12:00   13:00   14:00   15:00 0
01/15/03   01/16/03   01/17.

VOLUME AND THE S&P FUTURES

- Volume is the train that pulls prices in the direction of your trade.
- Volume usually increases at the open and close and seems to dry up at lunchtime.
- If volume is increasing, the price trend will usually continue.
- If volume is decreasing and price is increasing, the trend could reverse.
- If volume is decreasing the price trend will decrease or consolidate.

Figure 10

SINGLE BAR PATTERNS

Wide Range Bars

- A wide range bar is a lot larger than the previous bars.
- A wide range bar represents a significant increase in volatility.
- Before trading a wide range bar, a trader needs to determine the trend of the market and how the wide range bar opened and closed.
- If the market is in an uptrend, a wide range bar may suggest a continuation of the trend if the bar closes on its high. A lower close suggests that the trend may not continue and could reverse.
- If a downtrend is in place, a wide range bar may suggest a continuation of the trend if the bar closes on its low. A higher close suggests that the trend may not continue and could reverse.
- A period of short consolidation can occur after a wide range bar before the trend continues.

Outside Range Bars

- Outside bars have a higher high and lower low than the previous bar.
- Volatility increases and the outside range bar completely extends above and below the previous bar (Figure 11).
- If the outside bar closes in the opposite direction of the trend with increased volume, a reversal is suggested.
- The outside range bar has more significance if the bar has a range larger than the previous 3 to 4 bars and/or it closes above the highs (or below the lows) of the last 3 to 4 bars.

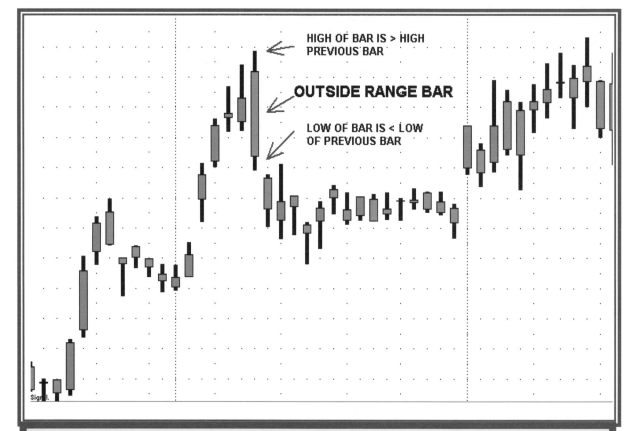

OUTSIDE RANGE BARS
S&P E-MINI 5 MINUTE CHART
- The range bar extends above and below the previous bar.
- If the outside range bar closes in the opposite direction of the trend with increased volume, a reversal is suggested.
- The bar has more significance, if the bar has a range greater than the previous three or four bars and/or it closes above the highs (or below the lows) of the last there to four bars.

Figure 11

Inside Range Bars

- The high of the present bar is less than high of previous bar and the low of the present bar is greater than the low of the previous bar (Figure 12).
- Volatility is decreased and can lead to a breakout trade.
- The ID/NR4 (Inside day, Narrow Range, 4 Days) was described by Toby Crabel as a breakout trade based upon inside bars.
- Small price bars tend to trend and large bars tend to reverse

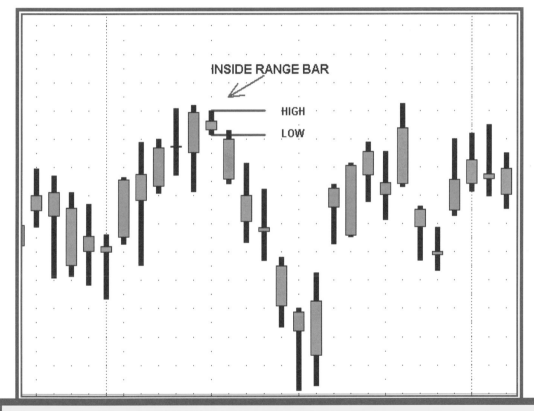

INSIDE RANGE BARS
MICROSOFT DAILY CHART

- The range of the inside bar is less than the range of the previous bar.
- Volatility is decreased and can lead to a breakout trade.
- This bar has the smallest range of the last 10 bars, which suggests the possibility of a greater move to the upside or downside.
- A trader needs to place a buy stop at the high and sell stop at the low of the bar to enter the trade, since it is hard to pick the right direction of the move.
- Small price bars tend to trend, which gives the trader a greater chance of profits.
- Large price bars tend to reverse.

Figure 12

BREAKOUT TRADES

Prior to March of 2000, breakout trading was a very popular trading strategy. A trader could buy on the breakout of a high or above resistance and the strategy usually resulted in profits. This was a smooth ride with few whipsaws. After the technology meltdown, the road to riches became very bumpy. This has required traders to come up with new strategies to beat the markets. The previous momentum traders are nearly extinct and their followers have seen losses rather than profits.

The problem today is that momentum is here one minute and gone the next. If you buy just above the high of the day, the sensation is like someone has pulled the plug out of the bathtub. The prices seem to reverse immediately with no follow through. The average daily range has decreased dramatically since March 2000. In the past, a $100 stock might have a range of 10 points per day. Now, it may only have a daily range of 50 cents to a dollar. This is partly due to decreased volume and the fact that stocks are trading at much lower prices.

Another factor that has contributed to breakout failures has been that markets are more efficient. Powerful computers and trading software are giving all traders an opportunity to be successful in the trading game. This has created the 'crowd effect' where numerous traders are buying and selling at the same location on a chart. This causes traders to try to enter the trade a little earlier than everyone else. This has caused traders to learn other strategies like reversal trades that are described below.

REVERSAL TRADES - BAR CHARTS

Numerous traders have felt the sting of disappointment when prices look like they are ready to take-off, but instead sputters and reverses. The first instinct is to take your losses and run. However, some traders are reversing their positions and trading false signals.

DOUBLE TOP (M pattern)

- See new high (First Peak), followed by correction (retracement).
- This is followed by second high near the first high and followed by a second reversal and sell off.
- Support is the retracement between the two highs.
- A Double top is confirmed when prices fall below the support that confirms the uptrend has ended.
- Must occur after a trend of some length to be effective. Dual peaks in a trading range or volatile market are not good trades.
- Enter short sale below support of Double Top. (Figure 13)

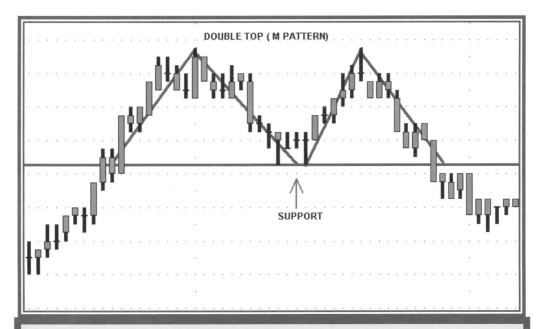

DOUBLE TOP (M PATTERN)

SUPPORT

REVERSAL TRADES – DOUBLE TOP
S&P E-MINI 5 MINUTE CHART
- See double peaks in M pattern followed by reversal and sell off.
- Confirmed when prices fall below support and uptrend has ended.
- Must occur after trend. Not reliable in non-trending trading range.
- Sell short below support.

Figure 13   41

DOUBLE BOTTOM (W pattern)

- See new low (first dip), followed by correction (retracement)
- This is followed by second low near the first low and followed by second reversal.
- Support is the retracement between the two lows.
- A double bottom is confirmed when prices rise above support that confirms the downtrend has ended.
- Must occur after a trend to be effective. Dual bottoms in a trading range or volatile market are not good trades.
- Enter buy order above support (Figures 14).

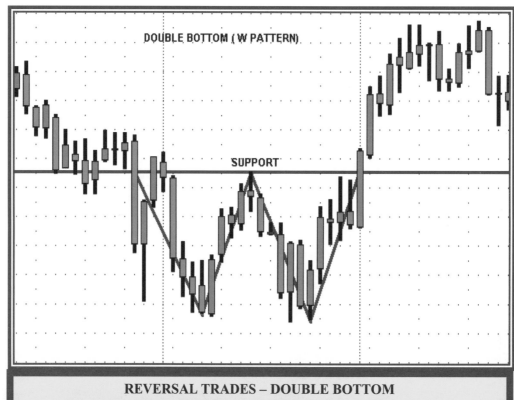

REVERSAL TRADES – DOUBLE BOTTOM
- Support is retracement between the two lows.
- Double bottom is confirmed when prices rise above support.
- Most reliable if prices are in trend. Avoid in trading ranges.
- Enter buy order above support.

Figure 14

SPIKES (V formations) AT PRICE TOPS

- A spike results in a sudden trend reversal without warning.
- Major selling is taking place.
- More significant if it occurs after a major advance.
- If you see 2 or more spikes, this is more ominous sign of heavy selling. Get out of the trade as soon as possible and consider going short. (Figure 15)

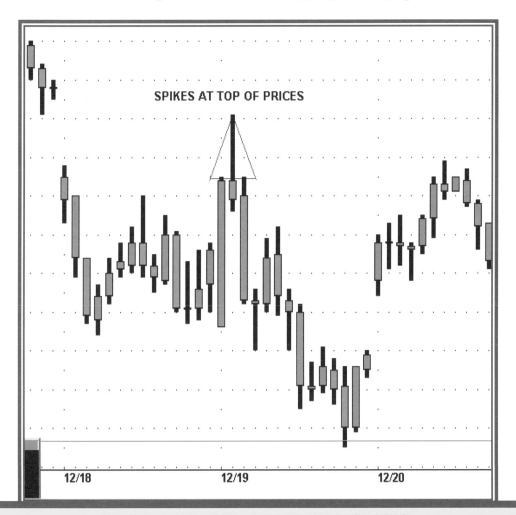

REVERSAL TRADES – SPIKES AT PRICE TOPS
- Trend can reverse without warning.
- Major selling is occurring. If you have bought futures, get out as quickly as possible.
- Most significant if it occurs at the end of a trend.
- If you see two or more spikes, it is an even more ominous sign of heavy selling.

Figure 15

SPIKES (V formations) AT PRICE BOTTOMS

- A spike suggests a trend reversal at the bottom
- Major buying is taking place.
- Most significant if it occurs after a major decline
- If you see 2 or more spikes there is serious buying coming into the market. You need to exit short positions and consider going long. (Figure 16)

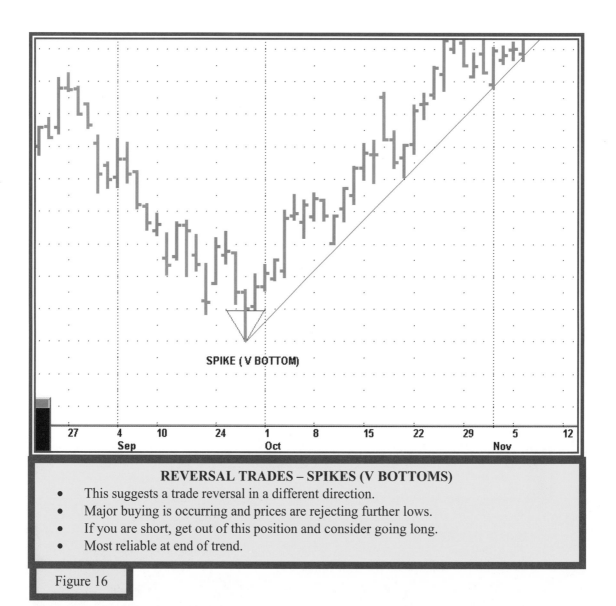

SPIKE (V BOTTOM)

27 4 10 24 1 8 15 22 29 5 12
Sep   Oct   Nov

REVERSAL TRADES – SPIKES (V BOTTOMS)
- This suggests a trade reversal in a different direction.
- Major buying is occurring and prices are rejecting further lows.
- If you are short, get out of this position and consider going long.
- Most reliable at end of trend.

Figure 16

PATTERN REVERSALS

Before the "Internet" revolution, access to information was limited for the amateur trader and the professional trader dominated the trading of specific price patterns. Today, the broad knowledge of trading patterns is available to everyone and it has helped to increase market efficiency. When everyone is trading the same pattern, that pattern loses its ability to make money. This has caused a lot of traders to move opposite of the crowd and trade reversals that will be more financially rewarding. The usual head-and-shoulder pattern is shown below (Figure 17) followed by a reversal trade with a head-and-shoulder pattern (Figure 18).

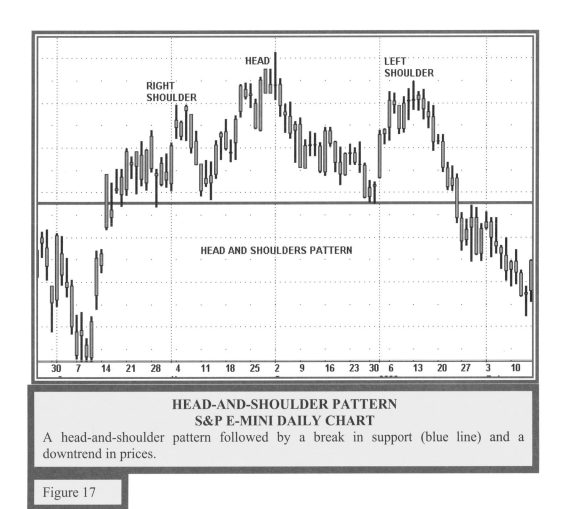

HEAD-AND-SHOULDER PATTERN
S&P E-MINI DAILY CHART
A head-and-shoulder pattern followed by a break in support (blue line) and a downtrend in prices.

Figure 17

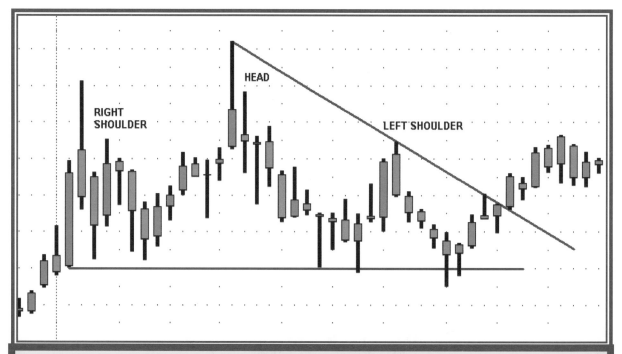

HEAD-AND-SHOULDER PATTERN
YAHOO WEEKLY CHART

- The chart shows the head-and-shoulder pattern breaking to the upside rather than to the usual down side. This is a market reversal and can fake a trader out.
- Trading against the crowd can be profitable.

Figure 18

MAJOR BEARISH REVERSAL SIGNALS - CANDLESTICK CHARTS

NRB (Narrow Range Bar) After Rally

- A bar with small range between high and low (Figure 19).
- Decreased volatility increases the chance of a reversal
- Greater chance of reversal if Narrow Range Bar occurs in trend or after rally
- Is a signal of the need to sell position or tighten stops

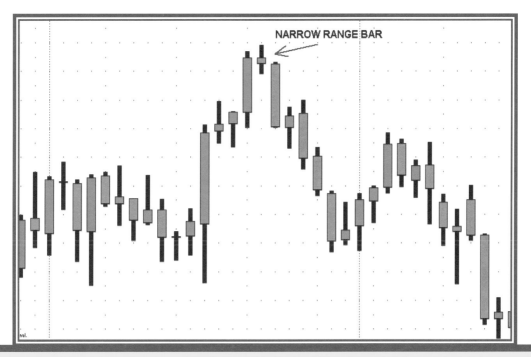

CANDLESTICK REVERSAL TRADES – NARROW RANGE BARS (NRB)
- A bar with a small range between high and low.
- It is more reliable if this occurs at end of a trend or rally.
- If a trader sees a Narrow Range Bar, he needs to get out of the position or tighten his stops to protect profits.
- In this example, the S&P E-Mini had a rally upward followed by a NRB. The NRB was followed by a reversal to the downside.

Figure 19

CANDLESTICK SPIKE OR TAIL

- Indicates major selling (Figure 20) or buying (Figure 21).
- Most significant if it is in the trend or rally
- If more than one spike occurs, it is an even stronger signal of selling and subsequent reversal (Figure 22).

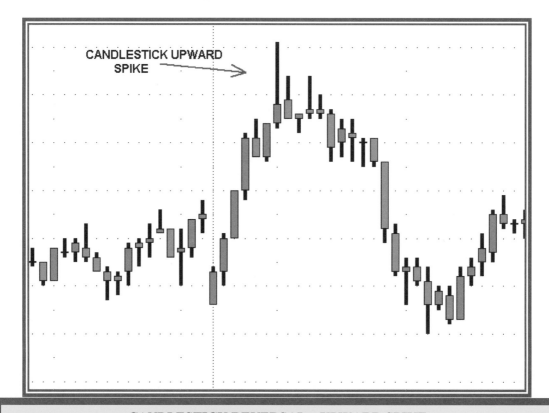

CANDLESTICK UPWARD SPIKE

CANDLESTICK REVERSAL – UPWARD SPIKE
- This indicates selling and reversal in prices.
- It is more significant if it occurs after a rally or in a trending market.
- This chart shows more than one spike at top of the rally, that is even stronger evidence for a reversal.

Figure 20

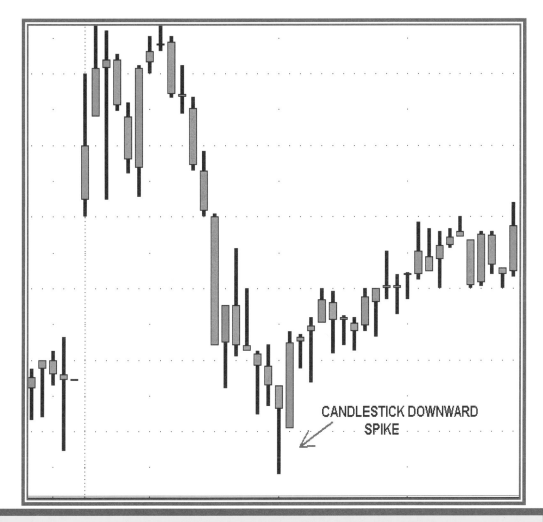

CANDLESTICK REVERSALS – DOWNWARD SPIKE

- Indicates major buying at a low.
- Prices are rejecting going any lower.
- Most significant if it occurs after a downtrend.

Figure 21

DOJI

- A 'Doji' is a candlestick pattern that opens and closes at or near the same price.
- Needs to be in a multi-bar rally to be significant.
- Looks like a cross or plus. (Figure 22)
- High of the 'Doji' can become resistance in a rally.
- Tighten stops or sell because prices could sink like the Titanic.

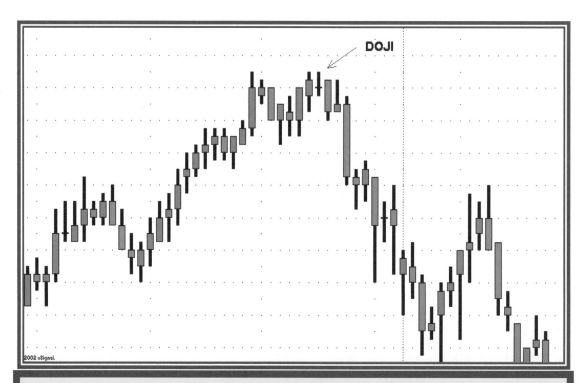

CANDLESTICK REVERSALS – DOJI
- The S&P E-Mini shows a nice uptrend until it forms a 'Doji.' We call this formation 'the Doctor of Death' sign because your trend may come to an abrupt ending.
- The 'Doji' is a candlestick that opens and closes at or near the same price.
- It is a small range bar like the previous Narrow Range Bar.

Figure 22

FAILED UPSIDE GAP

- See a gap above prior bar's high (Figure 23).
- Multi-bar advance prior to up gap
- Shortly after the gap up, the bar closes below the previous bar's high (fills the gap).
- Look to sell futures with a decent gap up in a multi-bar rally. Professional traders will try to sell into strength and fade the rally.

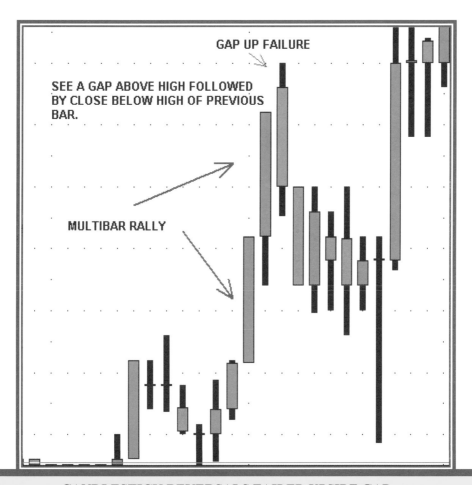

CANDLESTICK REVERSALS FAILED UPSIDE GAP
- There is a gap above previous bar's high followed by a close below the previous bar's high (fills the gap).
- More reliable with multi-bar advance before the gap up.
- Professional traders will sell the rally; while amateur traders will try to buy the breakout.

Figure 23

BEARISH CHANGING OF THE GUARD
(BCOG)

- A 'Bearish Changing of the Guard' is the same as 'Failed Upside Gap' without the gap.
- This is a less bearish signal than the 'Failed Upside Gap'
- See bullish multi-bar rally followed by a bar that closes below opening price (Figure 24)
- Best to sell when you see 'Bearish Changing of the Guard' after rally.

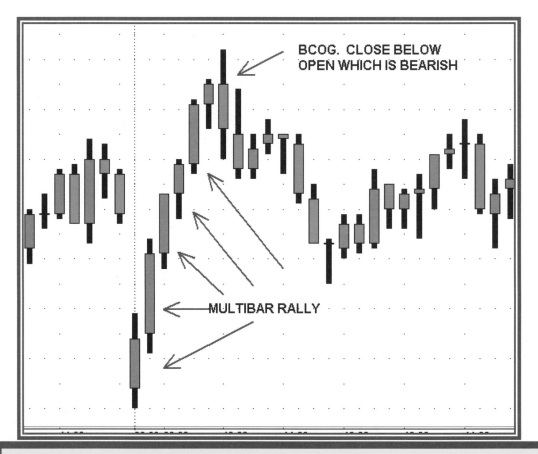

CANDLESTICK REVERSALS
BEARISH CHANGING OF GUARD (BCOG)
- For a close greater than the open, the bulls are in control and the candlestick body will be green.
- For a close less than the open, the bears are in control and the candlestick body will be red.
- The 'Bearish Changing of the Guard' is when you see a multi-bar bull rally followed by a close below the open which suggests the bears are again flexing their muscles.

Figure 24

Combination of
Narrow Range Bar and Bearish Changing of the Guard

- A combination of NRB and BCOG is an even stronger predictor of a trend reversal than a single signal.

OTHER REVERSAL SIGNALS - CANDLESTICK CHARTS

HARAMI

- A 'Harami' is a candle with a small body, which is inside the previous candle's body (Figure 25).
- It is usually the opposite color of the previous bar.
- The current trend is running out of steam and there is usually consolidation or correction coming.

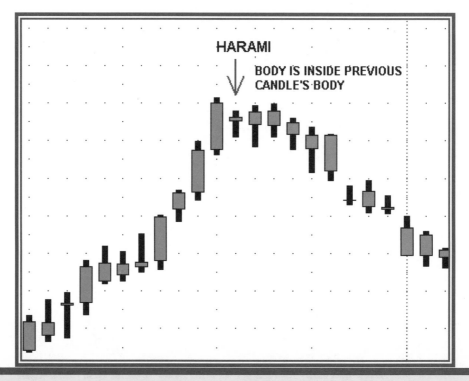

OTHER REVERSALS – CANDLESTICK CHARTS
HARAMI
- The body of the present candle is smaller than the previous candle's body.
- It means the bulls and bears are in tug-of-war and there is no winner for that day.
- This signal is usually followed by a consolidation or a change in trend.

Figure 25

BEARISH ENGULFING LINE

- A 'Bearish Engulfing Line' is a tall red candle that opens above and closes below the previous candle's real body (Figure 26).
- It seems to swallow up the previous candle.
- Suggests selling pressure.

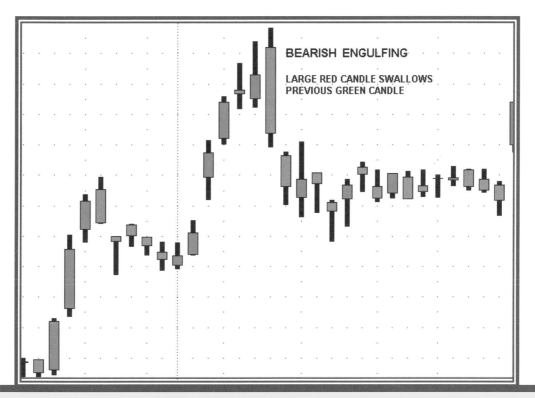

BEARISH ENGULFING

LARGE RED CANDLE SWALLOWS
PREVIOUS GREEN CANDLE

OTHER CANDLESTICK REVERSALS
BEARISH ENGULFING
- See the development of a large red candle in an uptrend that opens above and closes below the previous candle's real body.
- The candle seems to swallow up the previous candle's body.
- We call this the "bear hug" sign, since the bears are squeezing the life out of the bulls.

Figure 26

DARK CLOUD COVER

- 'Dark Cloud Cover' is a tall red candle that occurs in an uptrend.
- The open is above the previous candle's high
- The close is at least halfway down into the previous candle's body (Figure 27).
- 'Dark Cloud Cover' is a bearish sign

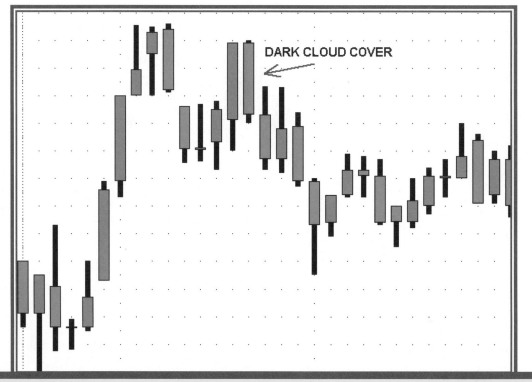

OTHER REVERSAL SIGNS – CANDLESTICKS – DARK CLOUD COVER
Red candle that opens above previous candle's high and closes at least halfway down into the previous candle's body.

Figure 27

SHOOTING STAR

- A 'Shooting Star' is a candle with a long upper shadow and a small body at the low end of the bar's range.
- Looks like a croquet mallet or sledge hammer (Figure 28).
- A 'Shooting Star' is a bearish reversal sign
- A 'Shooting Star' is more significant if it is present when the market is overbought

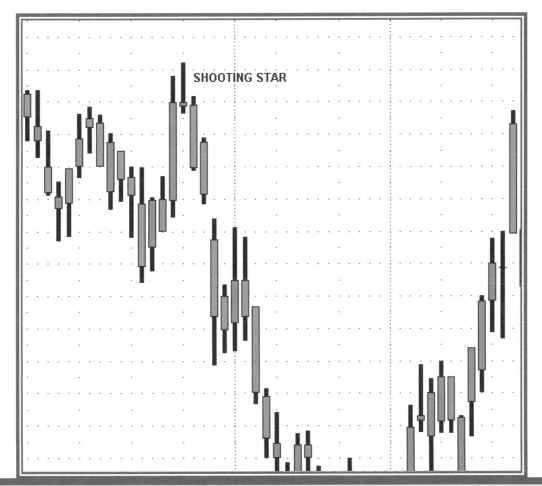

OTHER REVERSAL SIGNS
CANDLESTICKS – SHOOTING STAR
- Candle with a long upper shadow and a small body at the lower end of the bar's range
- More significant in overbought market

Figure 28

HANGING MAN

- A 'Hanging Man' looks like a 'Hammer' with a small body at the top of the range. There is a long shadow below the body that is 2-3 times the height of the real body (Figure 29).
- A 'Hanging Man' is most significant when it appears after a rally.
- A 'Hanging Man' is a bearish reversal sign.
- The market is rejecting higher prices.

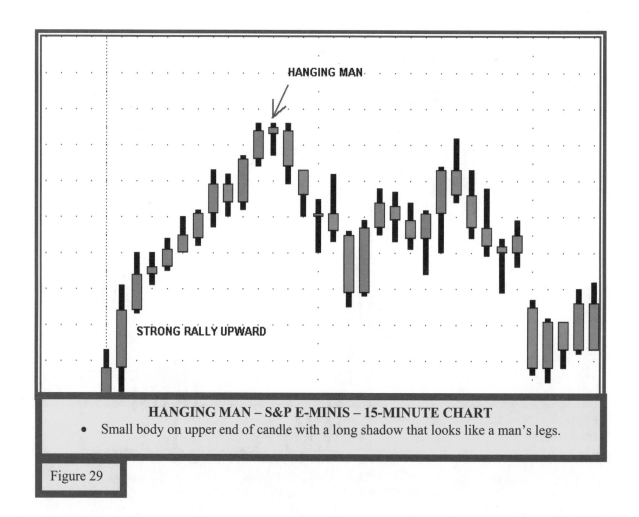

HANGING MAN – S&P E-MINIS – 15-MINUTE CHART
- Small body on upper end of candle with a long shadow that looks like a man's legs.

Figure 29

BULLISH ENGULFING PATTERN

- A 'Bullish Engulfing Pattern' is a tall green candle, which surrounds the body of the previous candle (Figure 30).
- This is a signal that occurs during a downtrend.
- It means that the bulls have taken control of price activity.

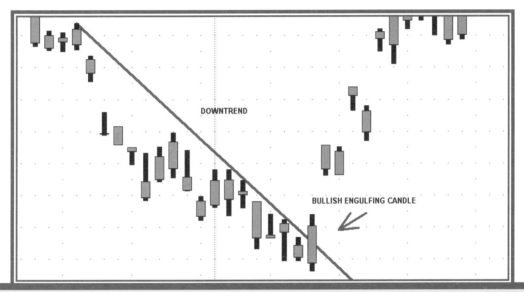

OTHER CANDLESTICKS – BULLISH ENGULFING PATTERN
IBM DAILY CHART
- Usually occurs at the end of a downtrend.
- It is a large green candle that completely engulfs the previous body of a small red candle.
- We call this the "bull hug candle," because the bulls are squeezing the life out of the bears.

Figure 30

HAMMER

- Looks just like a 'Hanging Man' in reverse (Figure 31).
- It is called a 'Hammer' and is most significant at the end of a downtrend. A 'Hanging Man' is most significant at the end of a rally.
- It indicates that the market is rejecting lower prices.

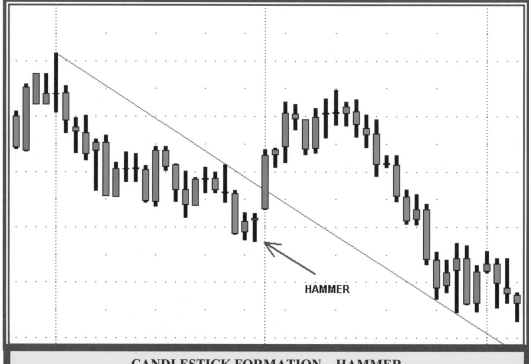

CANDLESTICK FORMATION—HAMMER
DAILY CHART OF S&P E-MINIS
- E-Minis are in a downtrend and a 'Hammer' forms
- The market reverses and rallies upward
- Notice how the 'Hammer' looks just like a 'Hanging Man.'

Figure 31

BULLISH DOJI

- A 'Doji' is a formation where the buyers and sellers are at a standstill.

- A 'Bullish Doji' can lead to a change in trend and looks like a plus sign (+) or 'T' (Figure 32).

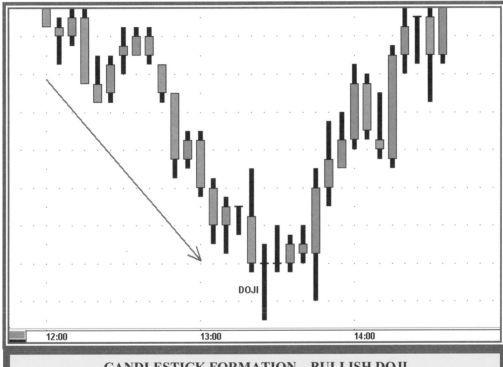

DOJI

12:00   13:00   14:00

CANDLESTICK FORMATION—BULLISH DOJI
S&P E-MINI 5 MINUTE CHART
- The chart shows a downtrend in prices where the market forms a 'Doji,' which is followed by an uptrend in prices.
- The Doji looks like a plus sign (+) or 'T.'

Figure 32

MORNING STAR BULLISH CANDLESTICK PATTERN

- The 'Morning Star Bullish Candlestick Pattern is' a three-candle pattern that usually occurs at market lows.
- It is made up of a bearish candle, a reversal type candle with a spike, which is then followed by a bullish candle (Figure 33).

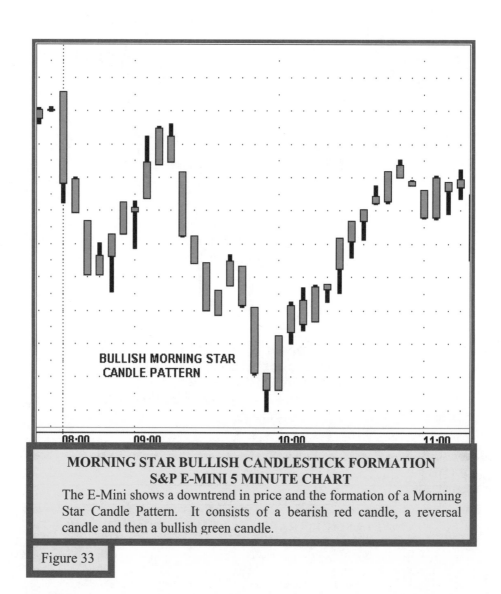

MORNING STAR BULLISH CANDLESTICK FORMATION
S&P E-MINI 5 MINUTE CHART
The E-Mini shows a downtrend in price and the formation of a Morning Star Candle Pattern. It consists of a bearish red candle, a reversal candle and then a bullish green candle.

Figure 33

CANDLESTICK TRAPS

- Trade candlestick signals when the market is at a bottom or top (Figure 34), but not in the middle of a move.
- Violating this rule will send you to the trader's cemetery.
- Never use candlesticks as your only indicator.

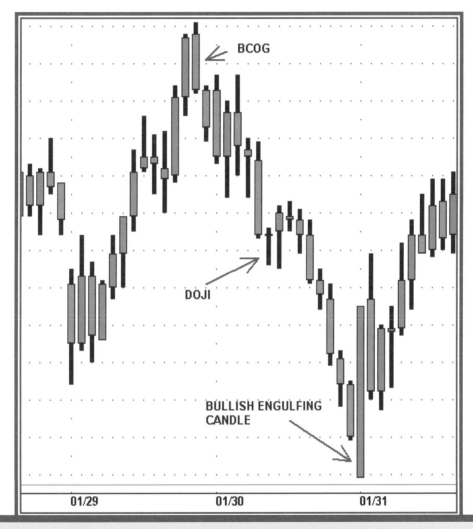

CANDLESTICK TRAPS – S&P E-MINI 10 MINUTE CHART
- A 'Doji' is present, which normally suggests a reversal in trend. Since the 'Doji' occurs in the middle of the down market, it is an unreliable signal. Candlesticks are best used as reversal tools at highs and lows.
- Notice the BCOG (Bearish Changing of the Guard) at the top of the rally which suggests a reversal and was followed by prices falling to new lows.
- A 'Bullish Engulfing Candle' is present at bottom of the down move.

Figure 34

SUMMARY OF CANDLESTICKS

- Candlestick formations reveal more information than bar charts.

- Candlestick signals may suggest a reversal more quickly than bar charts

- They may suggest market direction, before a trend develops.

- Candlesticks are best used after the market has trended up or down.

- Candlesticks can be misleading when used in the middle of rallies.

- The names can be confusing. In an uptrend, the candle can be called a 'Hanging Man,' but in a downtrend it can be called a 'Hammer.' A 'Harami' can be either a bullish or bearish signal depending upon whether it occurs at the top or bottom of a market move.

- Do not make trade decisions based only upon candlestick analysis. Look at other indicators to confirm market direction.

TIME AND SALES

The age-old tradition of tape reading was used in the 20th century to help determine whether the bulls or bears were in control of the market (Figure 35). The ability to watch the prices on a ticker tape has been replaced by time and sales screens on a computer. Time and sales show the actual trades that were executed, rather than just the 'bids' and 'offers' that are shown on the Level II screen. The following rules should be used when trading using time and sales.

- Don't rely on time and sales as a trading strategy. If time and sales shows buying, make sure there is evidence of higher price levels on the chart.

- Look to see if the majority of trades are occurring at the 'ask' price (green color) or 'bid' price (red color).

- If you see that the majority of trades are a green color at an increased transaction speed, this suggests increased buying pressure. Traders are having to chase the contracts and pay higher than the 'ask' price. It is like trying to jump onto a runaway train.

- If you see that the majority of trades are a red color at an increased transaction speed, this suggests increased selling pressure. Traders are not able to sell their contracts at the 'bid' price and must sell them for less to get out of the trade.

- If you see mixture of red and green (Christmas Tree Pattern), this is a sign to stay out of the trade.

Figure 35

MARKET INDICATORS THAT
SHOW STRENGTH AND WEAKNESS

(Breadth Indicators)

ADVANCE-DECLINE LINE

- The number of advancing stocks minus declining stocks that can offer a snapshot of market dynamics not revealed by price action.

  - If you see a strong downtrend in the advance-decline line, S&P prices will follow (Figure 36).

  - If you see a strong uptrend in the advance line, S&P prices will follow (Figure 37).

  - If the advance-decline line moves back and forth across the opening value, there is usually no momentum in either direction. The result is usually a flat, non-trending day (Figure 38).

- Advance-decline analysis is more commonly used to gauge long-term strength of the overall market, but it can be used to help with intra-day trading strategies.

E-Mini Prices	Advance-Decline Line	Interpretation
Increasing	Decreasing	Bearish
Decreasing	Increasing	Bullish

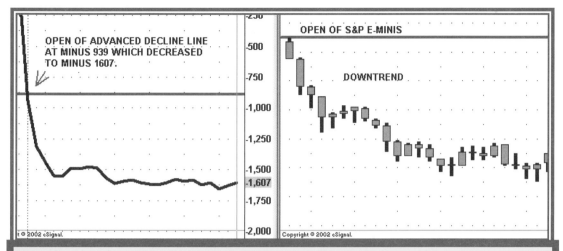

**CORRELATION OF ADVANCE/DECLINE LINE
S&P E-MINI – 15 MINUTE CHART**

- The advance-decline line shows a strong decline from the open, which was also evident in the S&P E-Mini chart.
- The advance-decline line can confirm price action in the S&P E-Mini.
- It is typically used by traders to look at long-term market strength.

Figure 36

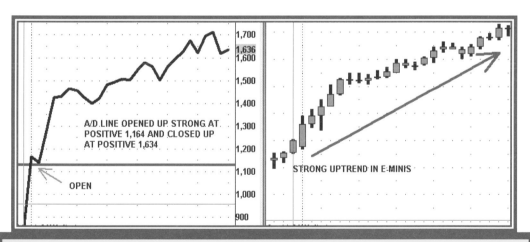

**CORRELATION OF ADVANCE-DECLINE LINE
S&P E-MINI**

- The advance-decline line opened up strong and advanced throughout the trading day. The E-Mini chart shows a similar strong uptrend.

Figure 37

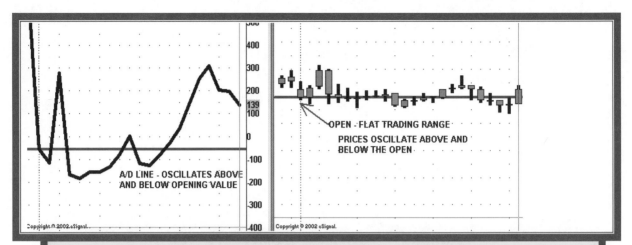

CORRELATION OF ADVANCE-DECLINE LINE
S&P E-MINI – 15 MINUTE CHART

- The advance-decline line can suggest a non-trending flat market.
- The advance-decline line opened at minus 56 and oscillates around the opening value. It only reached a positive value of 309. The S&P E-Mini chart showed a similar pattern where prices were in a flat trading range and hovered around the opening price throughout the day.

Figure 38

ADVANCE-DECLINE RATIO

The Advance-Decline Ratio is a market momentum indicator that involves the calculation of a ratio of advancing stock issues to the declining stock issues. The value is calculated over an established time period and the result is plotted as an oscillator.

- Formula = Advancing issues / (Advancing + Declining issues)

- The ratio will be greater than 0.5 when the advancing issues exceed the declining issues.

- The ratio will be less than 0.5 when declining issues are greater than advancing issues

- Take a 10-day moving average of the advance-decline ratio

    - Greater than 0.55 = Bullish

    - Less than 0.45 = Bearish

Short-Term Trading Index--TRIN

The Short-Term Trading Index is an index that quantifies the buying pressure relative to the selling pressure for the market as a whole.

1.   The Short-Term Trading Index (TRIN) indicates whether volume of trading is concentrated in advancing or declining issues.
2.   The formula is
       (Advancing issues/Declining issues) / (Advancing Volume/Declining volume)
3.   If advancing issues have increased volume, the signal is Bullish
4.   If declining issues have increased volume, the signal is Bearish
5.   A **TRIN** reading of 1 is non-diagnostic because the ratio of advancing issues to declining issues is the same as the ratio of up volume to down volume.
6.   Value > 1 = Bearish (Figure 39).
7.   Value < 1 = Bullish (Figure 40).
8.   Extremely low or high readings are often indicative of overbought or   oversold market conditions.
9.   A 10-day moving average is often used to smooth the readings
      A.   The moving average moves opposite of prices. It increases when the market is decreasing and decreases when the market is increasing.
      B.   The market is considered overbought when the 10 day moving average of TRIN is < 0.8 (Time to Sell). (Figure 41).
      C.   The market is considered to be oversold when the 10 day moving average of **TRIN** is > 1.2 (Time to Buy)
      D.   Must be interpreted in regards to the present market trend. A bullish market can be overbought for a long period of time and a bearish market can be oversold for a long period of time (Figure 42).

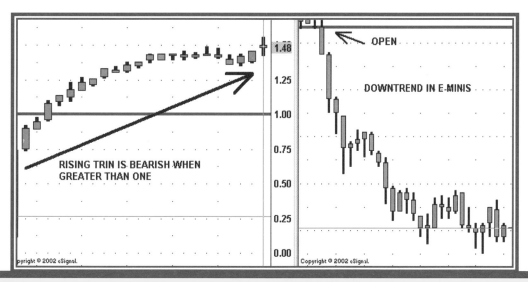

CORRELATION OF THE TRIN AND THE S&P E-MINI
15 MINUTE CHART
- A TRIN reading greater than one is considered bearish, which is confirmed in the E-Mini chart showing a downtrend in prices.
- TRIN of one is a neutral reading. Greater than one is bearish and less than one is bullish.

Figure 39

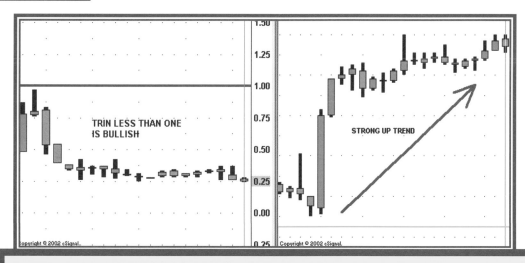

CORRELATION OF TRIN AND S&P E-MINI
15 MINUTE CHART
- If the TRIN reading is less than one, this is interpreted as bullish.
- The S&P E-Mini chart showed a strong uptrend when the TRIN was less than one.
- The TRIN helped to confirm the price trend.

Figure 40

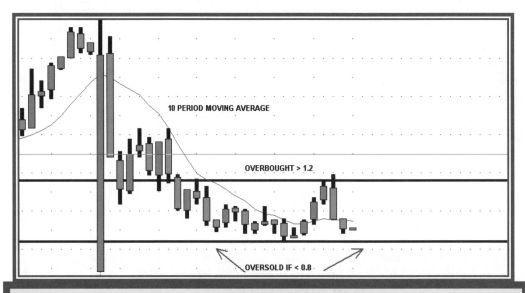

10 PERIOD MOVING AVERAGE OF TRIN
15 MINUTE CHART

- The market is overbought with a TRIN value of less than 0.8 (Time to sell).
- The market is oversold with a TRIN value greater than 1.2. (Time to buy).
- Exceptions are a strong bull or bear market which can remain overbought or oversold for a long period of time.

Figure 41

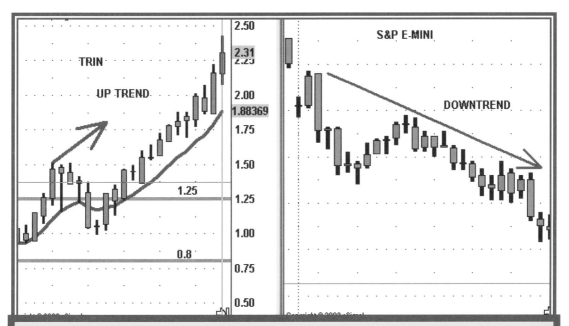

COMPARISON OF OVERSOLD TRIN AND S&P E-MINI
15 MINUTE CHART
- Chart on left shows the TRIN is oversold with a reading greater than 1.25
- The chart on the right shows the S&P E-Mini continuing to decline with an oversold reading on the TRIN. In a strongly trending market, the value can remain oversold while prices continue to trend downward.
- A trader should never trade against a strong trend. It can be compared to stepping in front of a train and hoping that you do not get hurt.

Figure 42

- TICK is the net difference between the number of stocks whose most recent trade occurred on an up tick and the number of stocks whose most recent trade occurred on a down tick. It is a most recent representation of net advancing issues.

- TICK shows the market's up and down momentum.

- Up-trending TICK is bullish (Figure 43).

- Down-trending TICK is bearish

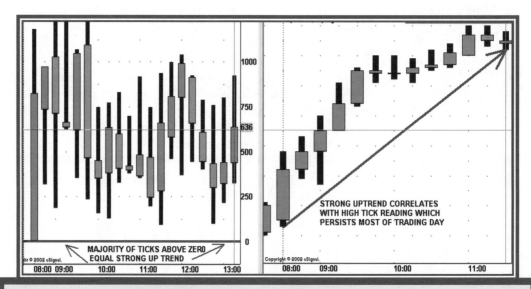

COMPARISON OF TICK AND S&P E-MINI CHART
- Uptrending TICK is bullish, especially when the value stays above the zero line and has values greater than 800.
- The TICK is volatile and should not be used as a sole indicator. Confirm the TICK with price and other indicators.

Figure 43

TICK analysis can confirm a trade before buying or selling the E-Mini contract. Taking a long position would be confirmed if the TICK was turning positive or accelerating to the upside. Taking a short position would be confirmed if the TICK was turning negative or accelerating to the downside. Beware that the TICK can have negative readings even in strongly uptrending markets (Figure 44) and can have positive readings in strongly downtrending markets (Figure 45). The important thing is to recognize if the majority of ticks are above or below the zero line. The TICK is not the perfect indicator and can show strong positive or negative readings with little movement in the S&P E-Mini chart (Figure 46).

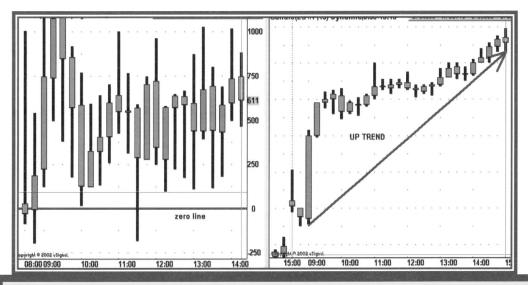

COMPARISON OF TICK CHART TO S&P E-MINI CHART
- In most cases, the TICK will cross over the zero line and give negative values even in strongly uptrending markets. The TICK chart on the left gives a minus reading of 200 with positive tick values of greater than 1000.
- Notice how the majority of ticks are in positive territory above the zero line.

Figure 44

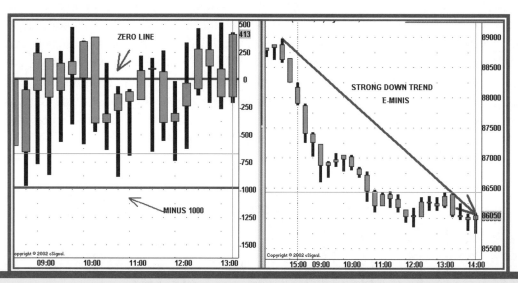

COMPARISON OF TICK CHART TO S&P E-MINI CHART
- The TICK nearly reached minus 1000 and the E-Mini chart showed a strong downtrend.
- Note that the TICK had a positive value of > 400 in a strong downtrend.
- The TICK is not as good as price in indicating the direction of the market.

Figure 45

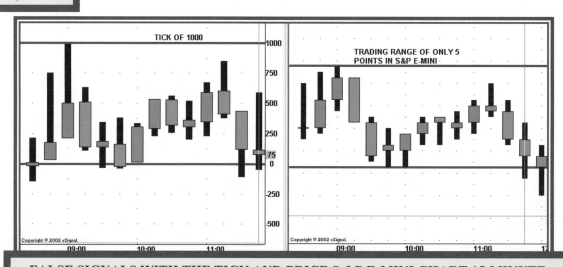

FALSE SIGNALS WITH THE TICK AND PRICE S &P E-MINI CHART 15-MINUTE
- The TICK showed a positive value of nearly 1000, which would usually be a sign of strength. The S&P E-Mini rallied 2 points with high TICK values and reversed to the downside.
- Trying to trade based upon solely the TICK is a sure way to end up in the trader's cemetery.

Figure 46

The TICK typically falls in a range between +600 and −600. We have found this to vary in the present trading environment. The TICK is like taking a single snapshot of the market and can be very volatile. Because of this, the TICK is sometimes smoothed with a 10 period moving average.

The TICK can be correlated with the TIKI and TRIN to support a long or short position in the market. When the indicators align, a trade has a greater chance of being successful.

In the example, there is a divergence between price and the TICK. The E-Mini S&P makes a new high, but the TICK makes a lower high. This suggests that momentum is falling and can result in a consolidation or reversal (Figure 47). The opposite divergence can occur when the TICK value is increasing and the market is flat. (Figure 48).

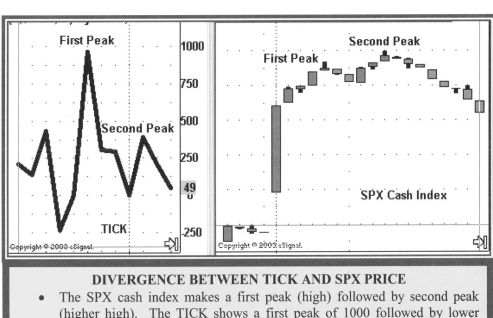

DIVERGENCE BETWEEN TICK AND SPX PRICE
- The SPX cash index makes a first peak (high) followed by second peak (higher high). The TICK shows a first peak of 1000 followed by lower second peak correlating with the second peak of the SPX. This illustrates a divergence between TICK and price. The lower TICK reading is followed by a decrease in prices.

Figure 47

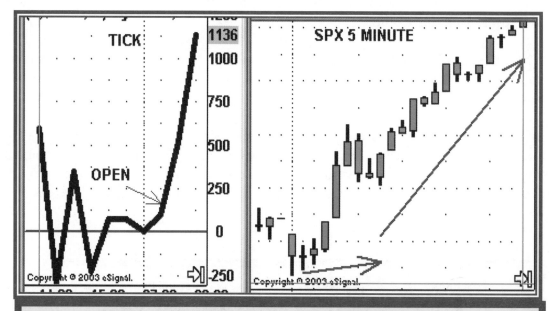

DIVERGENCE OF TICK AND S&P 500 CASH INDEX (SPX)
- The SPX gaps down at the open followed by sideways movement.
- The TICK shows a strong uptrend at the open, diverging from the action of the SPX.
- The strong TICK is followed by a strong uptrend in the SPX.

Figure 48

Extreme high or low readings of the TICK can indicate an overbought or oversold market. When the TICK value goes to an extreme level, it can become a contrarian indicator. A 1000+ TICK value is hard to maintain and many traders sell the market short expecting a reversal to the downside. A TICK value of -1000 may suddenly reverse to the upside for a long trade. This may sound like an easy way to make money by selling the market short or buying long based upon extreme readings in the TICK. Unfortunately, if the bulls or bears are running that strongly, you had better get out of their way. Do not try to fade a strong move in the afternoon when the market is more likely to trend (Figure 49).

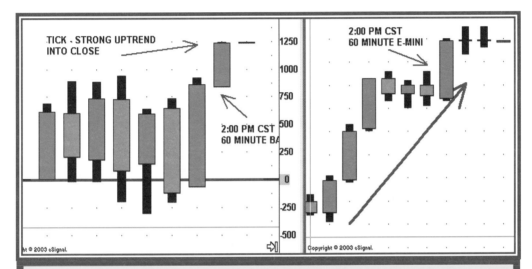

COMPARISON OF 60 MINUTE TICK AND E-MINI CHART
- The TICK at 2:00 pm CST has a value of +920. This reading suggests strong buying power in the afternoon. The E-Mini at 2:00 pm shows a strong upward trend into the close.
- The TICK tends to trend more often in the afternoon. It is not a good idea to fade a strong trend in the afternoon. A strong TICK value that is positive or negative in the afternoon is more likely to continue in that direction.

Figure 49

TICK DOUBLE TOP
(M pattern) Sell Signal

- Look for a double top on the S&P E-Mini chart.

    ■ Make sure the second top does not exceed the first top by 2.5 points.
    ■ The TICK needs to be greater than +600 for the first top.
    ■ The value of the TICK for the second top can be higher or lower, but has a higher probability of success if it is greater than +600.
    ■ Look for bearish reversal candlestick formations that were described in the previous section.

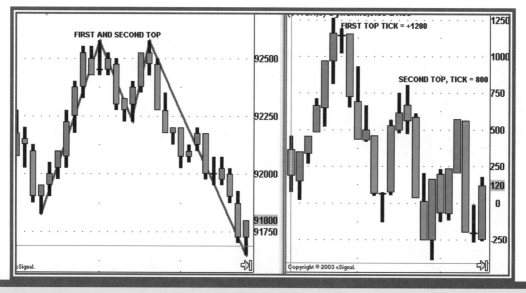

3 MINUTE S&P E-MINI CHART ON LEFT AND 3 MINUTE TICK CHART ON RIGHT
- The E-Mini chart shows a double top (M pattern). The second top does not exceed the first top by 2.5 points.
- The first top has a TICK value of + 1200 and the second top has a value of +800. Both values are greater than +600.
- Bearish candlestick patterns are present at both the first and second tops.

Figure 50

TICK DOUBLE BOTTOM
(W pattern) Long Signal

- Look for a double bottom on the S&P E-Mini chart.

    - Make sure the second bottom does not exceed the first bottom by more than 2.5 points.
    - The TICK needs to be strongly negative on the first bottom. The trade has a greater chance of success of the value is less than –800. We have used smaller numbers when the double bottom occurs after a downtrend.
    - The TICK value for the second bottom of the double bottom can be greater or less than the first. The lower the value is, the better the chances of success.
    - Look for the bullish candlestick reversal patterns that have been described in the previous sections.

- **Up-ticking Issues minus Down-ticking issues**

    - The TIKI has the same characteristics as the TICK, except that it is calculated on the 30 Dow stocks.
    - The TIKI plots on a scale of –30 to +30.
    - The TIKI can help identify huge buy and sell programs that occur with program trading on a daily basis (Figure 51).
    - If the TICK is greater than +1000 or less than -1000 with a TIKI that is beyond 22 (either positive or negative), it is likely that program trading is ruling the market at that time.
    - A TIKI of +26 or –26 has been reported as a good signal to fade the move. Remember that this rule will not always work, since a strong trend can occur 30% of the time.

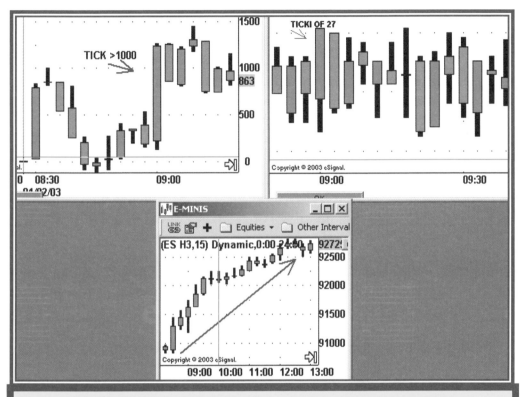

CORRELATION OF TICK AND TIKI IN PROGRAM TRADING

- When the TICK is greater than +1000, look at the value of the TIKI at the same time. If the TIKI is greater than 22, program buying is suggested.
- The upper left chart shows a TICK of +1250 and the right upper chart shows a TIKI of +27. These two values result in a strong uptrend in the E-Mini market, which is shown in the bottom chart.

Figure 51

52-WEEK NEW HIGHS MINUS 52-WEEK NEW LOWS

- 52 Week analysis can be used to assess the strength of the market trend.

- In a bull market, the number of stocks that are making new 52 week highs would be greater than the number of stocks making new 52 week lows.

- In a bear market, the number of stocks making new 52 week lows would be greater than the number of stocks making new 52 week highs.

- If the market continues to move higher but the number of stocks making new 52 week highs decreases, it is a sign that the trend is losing momentum and could reverse (Bearish Divergence).

- If the market continues to move lower but the number of stocks making new 52 week highs increases, it is a sign that the trend is losing momentum and could reverse (Bullish Divergence)

- Plot the 10-day moving average of 52-Week New Highs minus 52 Week New Lows.

- The indicator will move above and below the zero line.

  - When the average is above the line, the bulls are in control of the market and would be a confirmation of buying the market.

  - If the average is below the line, the bears are in control of the market and would confirm selling short.

52-WEEK NEW HIGHS DIVIDED BY 52-WEEK NEW LOWS

- A value greater than 1 is Bullish with more new highs than lows

- A value less than 1 is Bearish with more new lows than highs

- Use this indicator to confirm a bullish or bearish trend.

- Look for bullish and bearish divergence.

MARKET TRADING INDICATORS

MOVING AVERAGES (MA)

- A moving average is the average price of a futures contract over time. There are several different methods to calculate moving averages as outlined below.

- When prices rise above their moving average, it is bullish and is a good time to buy. When prices fall below their moving average, this is bearish and is a good time to sell.

- The moving average tends to keep the trader on the right side of the market during uptrends and downtrends. When the market moves sideways, a trader tends to get whipsawed by the market and lose money (Figure 52).

- Try to buy or sell the market near the moving average where true value exists. Traders who buy or sell far from the moving average are like the traders who buy the tops and/or sell the bottoms and wonder why they continue to lose money.

- In uptrending markets, go long when prices pull back to the moving average (Figure 53).

- In downtrending markets, go short when prices rally back to the moving average (Figure 54).

- Moving average crossovers have long been a popular simple trading system. A buy signal is generated when the shorter term moving average crosses above the longer term moving average. A sell signal is generated when the shorter term moving average crosses below the longer term moving average (Figure 55). Moving average crossovers work well in a trending market, but are ineffective when the market is stuck in a trading range. This causes numerous false buy and sell signals. Moving average crossovers can be used effectively in trading when combined with other indicators.

- The major difference between the different types of moving averages is the weight assigned to the most recent data.

  - Simple MA - Applies equal weight to all prices
  - Exponential and Weighted Averages apply more weight to recent prices.
  - Triangular MA - Apply more weight to prices in middle of period.
  - Variable MA - Based upon volatility of prices
  - Volume adjusted MA - Based upon volume of period.

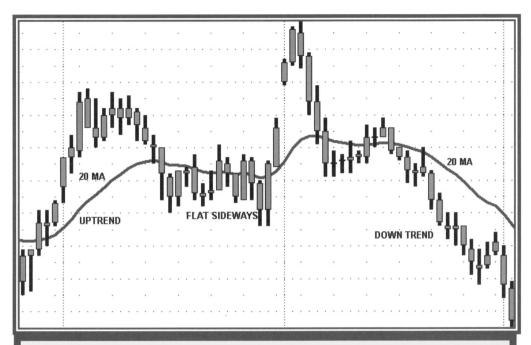

S&P E-MINI
15 MINUTE AND 20 PERIOD MOVING AVERAGE

- The blue line is a 20 period moving average. It initially rises and then goes sideways followed by a downtrend.
- When the market price is above the moving average, it is bullish
- A sideways moving average is a sign to stay out of the market and do not trade.
- When the market is below the moving average, it is bearish.

Figure 52

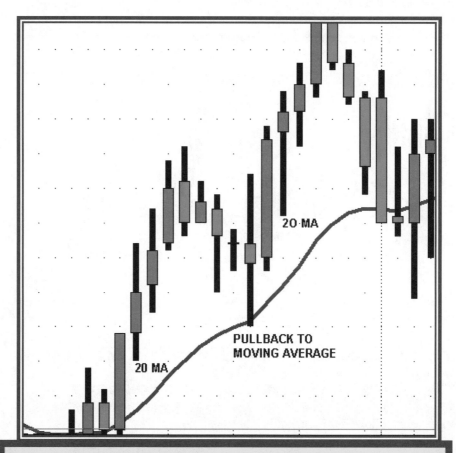

S&P E-MINI— 5 MINUTE CHART
PULLBACK TO 20 PERIOD MOVING AVERAGE
The E-Mini shows a move above the 20 period moving average (Bullish).
The prices pull back to the 20 period moving average. This is a good place
to enter a position in an uptrend.

Figure 53

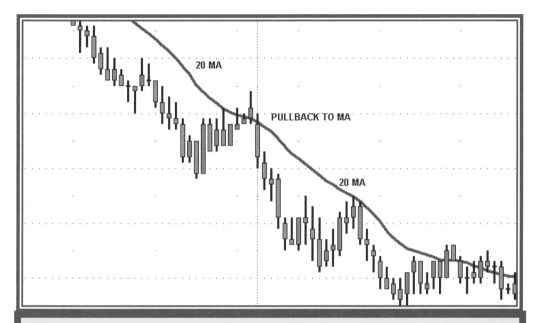

S&P E-MINI—5 MINUTE CHART
DOWNTREND WITH PULLBACK TO 20 PERIOD MOVING AVERAGE
The E-Mini market is in a downtrend and shows two episodes of moving back to the moving average. These are good entry places for short positions.

Figure 54

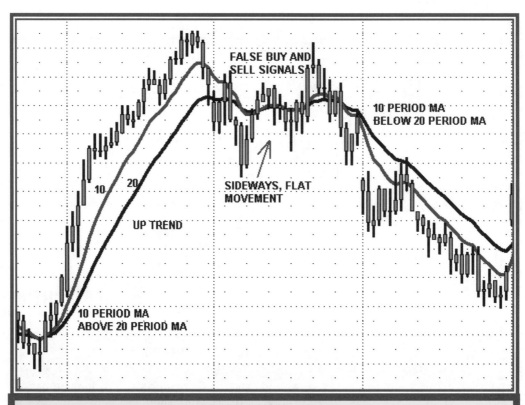

MOVING AVERAGE CROSSOVER
S&P E-MINI 15-MINUTE CHART
- The E-Mini market shows an initial uptrend followed by sideways movement and a subsequent downtrend.
- The blue line (10 period moving average) crosses above the black line (20 period moving average) and gives a buy signal early in the uptrend.
- When the E-Mini shows sideways movement, the blue line crosses back and forth across the black line and gives numerous false buy and sell signals.
- The E-Mini market goes into a downtrend and the blue line crosses below the black line and gives a good sell signal. This chart strongly illustrates that a trend is needed to successfully trade a moving average crossover strategy.

Figure 55

KELTNER CHANNELS

Keltner channels are bands that establish boundaries for a market's price fluctuations. The original Keltner bands were constructed using the high, low and close of each bar and then calculating a 10-period moving average of these values. Most programs like E-Signal use a later version of the channel calculation that was popularized by Raschke. This calculates an exponential moving average of price. The upper and lower bands are created by adding and subtracting a multiple of the average true range (ATR). Keltner channels can reflect changes in volatility. When the average true range (ATR) is high, the volatility is high. When the average true range (ATR) is low, the volatility is low. A close above the upper Keltner band (Figure 56) or below the lower band (Figure 57) represents strong momentum and should be traded as a breakout trade in that direction if confirmed by other indicators.

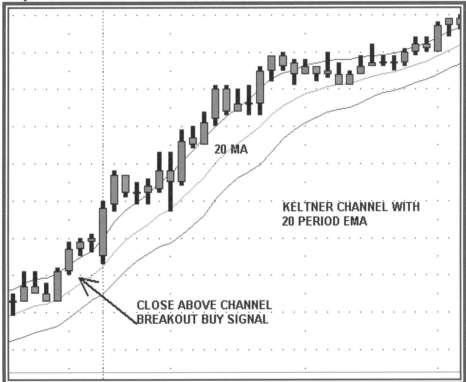

KELTNER CHANNEL AND UPTRENDING MARKET
S&P E-MINI 5 MINUTE CHART
- The E-Mini shows a strong uptrend in prices and the black arrow points to the first close above the Keltner channel. This is a breakout buy signal. Notice the continued uptrend after the breakout.
- The prices hug close to the upper band in a strongly uptrending market. The retracement back to the moving average represents a good buy point.

Figure 56

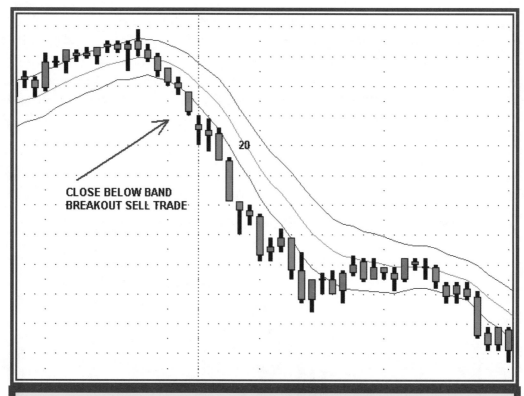

**KELTNER CHANNEL AND DOWNTRENDING MARKET
S&P E-MINI 5 MINUTE CHART**
1. The E-Mini market shows a strong downtrend and the blue arrow points to a close below the Keltner band. This is a breakout sell signal.
2. Notice how prices hug the lower band in a strongly downtrending market.

Figure 57

BOLLINGER BANDS

- Bollinger bands are price envelopes usually drawn two standard deviation units above and below a 20 period moving average (Figure 58).

- The width of the upper and lower lines of the price envelope are based upon volatility. When volatility increases, the Bollinger bands spread wide apart. This indicates increased upward and downward price movement or volatility. As volatility continues to decrease, the Bollinger bands become more narrow and the price action moves sideways.

- A price breakout tends to occur when the Bollinger bands contract and volatility decreases.

- When prices move outside of the band, it indicates that the trend will continue.

- A move that originates at one end of the band tends to continue to the other end of the band. This can be used as a method to project price targets.

- Since Bollinger bands involve volatility, they can also be used to analyze price information to trade options. Option pricing is based on volatility. A trader needs to buy options when volatility is low and sell options when volatility is high.

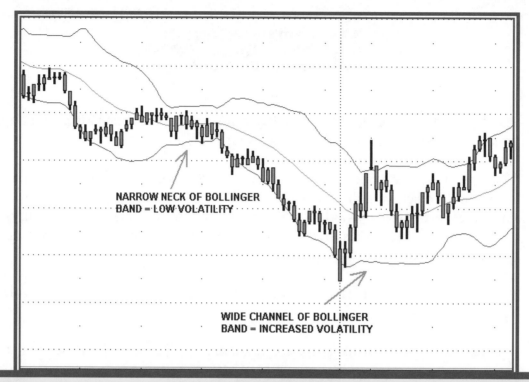

BOLLINGER BANDS
S&P E-MINI 15 MINUTE CHART
- When the Bollinger band narrows, the volatility decreases and sets the stage for a breakout in prices. This chart shows a narrow neck in the Bollinger band, which leads to a strong downtrend in prices.
- The wide channel represents increased volatility where there is greater up and down price movements.

Figure 58

AVERAGE TRUE RANGE
(ATR)

The normal standard range calculation is simply the high minus the low. The true range is a measure of price movement that takes into account gaps that occur between price bars and provides a more accurate picture of the size of the price move over a given period of time. The Average True Range (ATR) is simply a moving average of the true range over a certain period of time.

The true range is the greatest distance between:

- Today's high and today's low
- Today's high and yesterday's close
- Today's low and yesterday's close

The Average True Range (ATR) alone cannot provide a good prediction of market direction. It can be useful when you see an increase in values that can be seen with price movement. Average True Range (ATR) is a simple volatility calculation and it reflects the total price bar change from one bar to the next. The Average True Range (ATR) number will always be positive, because the smaller number (opening or closing) is subtracted from the larger number. A high Average True Range (ATR) number suggests a strongly trending market either up or down. A low number could indicate a consolidation, continuation of the present market direction, or a trend reversal (Figure 59 & 60).

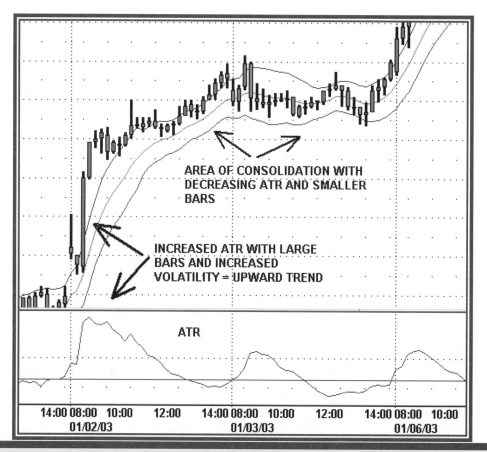

**CORRELATION OF AVERAGE TRUE RANGE AND PRICE
S&P E-MINI 15 MINUTE CHART**
- On Jan. 2, 2003, the E-Mini market opened with large bars and increased volatility (high ATR) which represents an upward trend.
- On Jan. 3, 2003, the E-Mini market has a consolidation phase with a decrease in the ATR. When the Average True Range decreases, it can lead to consolidation, a continuation move or a reversal.

Figure 59

AVERAGE TRUE RANGE
S&P E-MINI 15 MINUTE CHART
- An increasing Average True Range (ATR) can reflect an uptrend or downtrend as shown in this chart. The E-Mini in this chart is in a strong downtrend with an increasing ATR.

Figure 60

97

MOVING AVERAGE CONVERGANCE/DIVERGANCE

(MACD)

- The Moving Average Convergence/Divergence (MACD) is a momentum and trend following indicator that identifies overbought and/or oversold conditions. It is an indicator that oscillates above and below the zero line.

- MACD line consists of 3 moving averages that form 2 lines.

  - Fast or MACD line = (26-Day EMA minus 12-Day EMA)
  - Slow or signal line = (9-Day EMA of the fast line)
  - EMA = Exponential Moving Average

- It is recommended to buy when MACD line rises above the signal line and to sell when the MACD line falls below the signal line.

- Many traders buy when MACD rises above the zero line and sell when MACD falls below the zero line.

- Overbought and oversold conditions are evident when the shorter moving average pulls an impressive distance away from the longer term moving average.

- Divergence may indicate the end of the current trend. Bullish Divergence occurs when the MACD is making new highs and prices fail to reach new highs. Bearish Divergence is when MACD is making new lows and prices fail to make new lows.

- MACD lines follow trends and are a lagging indicator. They tend to generate buy and sell signals late. They tend to whipsaw in choppy markets that are non-trending. (Figure 61 & 62).

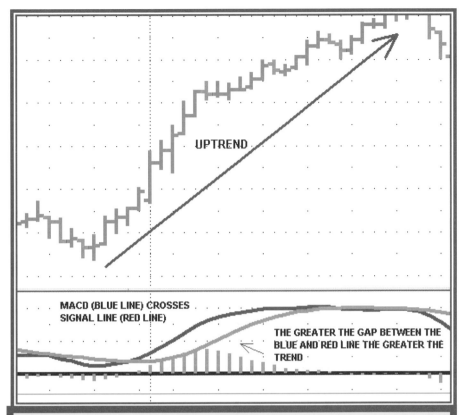

MOVING AVERAGE CONVERENCE/DIVERGENCE (MACD)
S&P E-MINI 15-MINUTE CHART
- The E-Mini market shows a strong uptrend. The MACD line crosses above the signal line generating a signal to buy E-Mini futures. Another buy signal could be generated when the MACD line crosses above the zero line.
- The trend is stronger as the distance between the MACD line and signal line gets larger. This chart shows an initial wide gap between the two lines, which narrows quickly as the trend comes to an end.

Figure 61

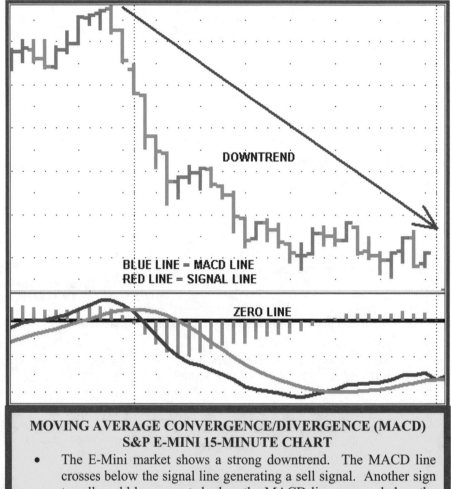

DOWNTREND

BLUE LINE = MACD LINE
RED LINE = SIGNAL LINE

ZERO LINE

**MOVING AVERAGE CONVERGENCE/DIVERGENCE (MACD)
S&P E-MINI 15-MINUTE CHART**

- The E-Mini market shows a strong downtrend. The MACD line crosses below the signal line generating a sell signal. Another sign to sell could be generated when the MACD line crosses below the zero line.
- This chart shows a wide initial gap between the two lines, which narrows quickly as the trend comes to an end.

Figure 62

MACD-HISTOGRAM

- Equal to fast MACD line (26-day EMA minus 12-day EMA) minus slow signal line (9-Day EMA of MACD line) (Figure 63).
- MACD Histogram measures the difference between the long and short term moving average and plots this value as a histogram.
- When the bars of the histogram rise, it means that the bulls are stronger. If the histogram declines sharply, the bears are stronger.
- Look for bullish and bearish divergence as described in the previous section.
- The crossovers between the signal line and the MACD line are equal to the histogram crossing the zero line

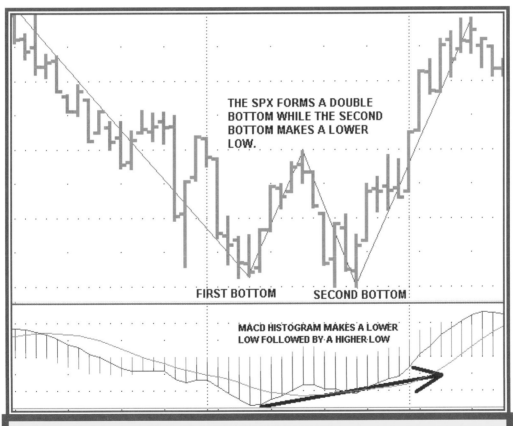

THE SPX FORMS A DOUBLE BOTTOM WHILE THE SECOND BOTTOM MAKES A LOWER LOW.

FIRST BOTTOM   SECOND BOTTOM

MACD HISTOGRAM MAKES A LOWER LOW FOLLOWED BY A HIGHER LOW

MACD DIVERGANCE
SPX DAILY CHART
- The SPX makes a double bottom with the second bottom making a lower low when compared to the first.
- The MACD histogram makes a lower low followed by a higher low. This represents a bullish divergence from prices. The market follows with an uptrend in prices.

Figure 63

PRICE OSCILLATORS (PO)

- Price oscillators are momentum indicators created to pinpoint market turning points and overbought/oversold levels.

- Price oscillators illustrate the emotional extremes of amateur traders. Professionals tend to fade those unsustainable levels of optimism and pessimism and bet that prices will return to normalcy. When the market rises on extreme unrealistic exuberance, such as with the Internet bubble, professional traders will try to sell right before the bubble bursts.

- When price oscillators are overbought, it indicates that prices are too high and ready to turn down. When price oscillators are oversold, prices are too low and ready to turn up.

- Price oscillators are sometimes called 'moving average oscillators' since they are formed from two moving averages. The price oscillator can be calculated by:

  - Subtract shorter moving average from longer moving average
  - (Shorter moving average - Longer moving average / Longer moving average) x 100

- In the price oscillator, the longer term moving average becomes the zero line and the shorter term moving average will cross above and below the zero line. The crossover of the shorter term moving average corresponds to a moving average crossover on a chart.

- Price oscillators work well in a trading range market, but are unreliable in a trending market. In a strongly trending bull market, a price oscillator can stay overbought indefinitely. In a strongly trending bear market, a price oscillator can stay oversold indefinitely.

- The best signals for a price oscillator are divergences.

  - Bullish divergence - Prices fall to new lows, while the price oscillator does not make a new low. This indicates the end of a downtrend.
  - Bearish divergence - Prices rise to new highs, while price oscillator does not make new highs. This indicates a market top, which is ready for a reversal (Figure 64).

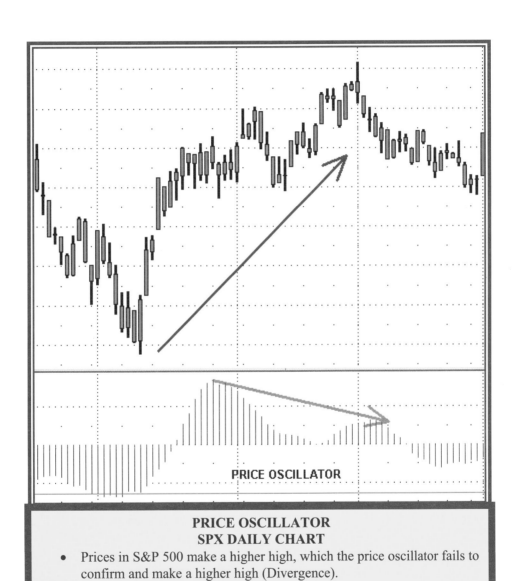

PRICE OSCILLATOR
SPX DAILY CHART
- Prices in S&P 500 make a higher high, which the price oscillator fails to confirm and make a higher high (Divergence).

Figure 64

STOCHASTIC OSCILLATORS

- The stochastic oscillator measures the position of the closing price for a market within a time interval. Prices tend to close at or near the extremes of their time period ranges during uptrends or downtrends.

- A stochastic oscillator helps avoid buying at high prices (overbought) or selling at low prices (oversold). It works like a warning light at a railroad   crossing to tell you not to chase a trend that is already overbought or oversold.

- There are two lines used in interpreting stochastic oscillators: fast and slow stochastics. The fast stochastic responds more rapidly to price changes and its lines are irregular. The slow stochastic is much smoother and easier to interpret.

- The 2 lines are composed of:

    - Main line (%K) – Displayed as a solid line and is the number of time periods used in the stochastic calculation.
    - Dotted line (%D) – Moving average of %K.

- Buy when the Main line (%K) falls below 20 and then rises above that level. Sell when it rises above 80 and then falls below that level. Some traders do not wait for the indicator to turn up to buy or turn down to sell. They will buy or sell when the stochastic indicator reaches an extreme level.

- Another signal from the stochastic oscillator is related to the direction of the lines of %K and %D. If both lines are moving up, they confirm a rising market. When %K crosses below % D (Figure 65), it may be an early warning signal that the market is ready to turn and move lower. If this crossover occurs when the stochastic lines are above the 80 reference line, a market turn may be more valid.

- Look for divergence between the stochastic oscillator and price.

- Do not use stochastic analysis alone because strongly trending markets cause the indicator to become quickly overbought or oversold (Figure 66). In a strongly trending market, the tendency is for the indicator to stay overbought or oversold for an indefinite period of time.

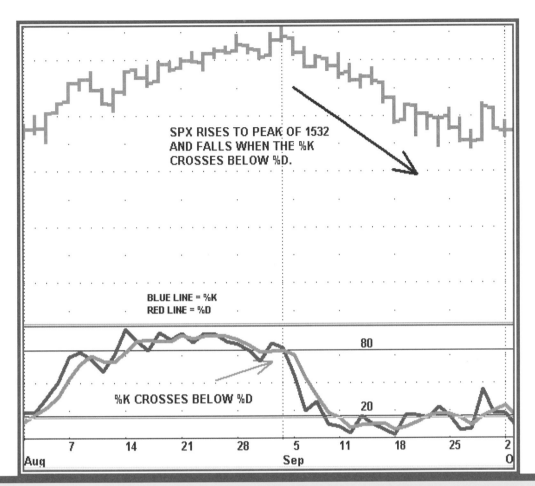

SPX RISES TO PEAK OF 1532
AND FALLS WHEN THE %K
CROSSES BELOW %D.

BLUE LINE = %K
RED LINE = %D

80

%K CROSSES BELOW %D

20

**STOCHASTIC OSCILLATOR—RISING MARKET
SPX DAILY CHART**

Upper chart shows the daily SPX making a new high at 1532. The %K crosses below %D and confirms the downtrend in prices.

Figure 65

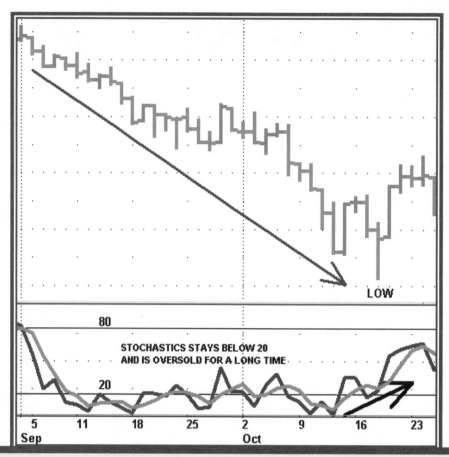

STOCHASTIC OSCILLATOR—FALLING MARKET
SPX DAILY CHART

- The SPX shows a strong downtrend while the stochastic oscillator shows it is oversold for a long period of time.
- The black arrow in the bottom chart illustrates a bullish divergence where the SPX makes a new low in price while the stochastic oscillator shows a higher low. This bullish divergence is followed by an uptrend in prices.

Figure 66

RELATIVE STRENGTH INDEX (RSI)

- The Relative Strength Index is a price oscillator that measures market strength by monitoring changes in closing prices.

- A top is identified when the RSI reaches a peak and turns down and a bottom is identified when the RSI falls and then turns up. Usually a peak value is over 70 and a bottom value is under 30.

- A divergence between price and the RSI gives the strongest buy and sell signals. As with other indicators, the divergence tells when the trend may reverse.

- Buy when the RSI goes below the lower reference line (30) and turns up. Sell when RSI goes above the upper reference line (70) and turns down.

- The RSI shows whether the bulls or bears were victorious at market closing time.

- The RSI can remain overbought or oversold while the trend continues (Figure 67).

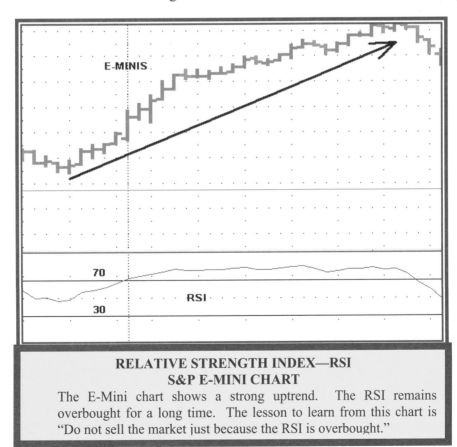

RELATIVE STRENGTH INDEX—RSI
S&P E-MINI CHART
The E-Mini chart shows a strong uptrend. The RSI remains overbought for a long time. The lesson to learn from this chart is "Do not sell the market just because the RSI is overbought."

Figure 67

107

AVERAGE DIRECTIONAL MOVEMENT INDEX (ADX)

- The ADX is designed to measure and graphically show the strength of a trend.
  - Strong trend - The higher the ADX value, the stronger the trend.
  - Weak trend - A lower ADX value, indicates a weak or non-existent trend.
  - ADX will increase in an uptrend or downtrend. ADX measures and shows trends, not trend direction.

- The ADX measures the difference between the Directional Movement plus (+DM) lines and Directional Movement minus (-DM) lines. This measures how much of the latest bar's price action falls outside of the previous bar's high and low readings.

- If +DM is above -DM, buy the market (Bullish). If -DM is above +DM, sell the market (Bearish).

- Best Buy signal, +DM and ADX are above -DM and ADX is increasing (Figure 68). Best Sell signal, -DM and ADX are above +DM and ADX is increasing (Figure 69).

- When the ADX value is greater than the +DM and –DM values, it indicates an overbought market.
  - When the ADX turns down, consider taking profits. Do not add to an existing position (Figure 70).

- A decreasing ADX, is not a trend.
  - ADX below +DM and –DM represents a flat non-trending market. (Figure 71).
  - It can be a strong signal if you see the ADX increase by 4 points in a flat market. This can be a sign that a new trend may be starting.

- The ADX is always a positive number. The ADX does not indicate the direction of the market. AN ADX value greater than 25 suggests that the market is trending. The trend can be up or down.

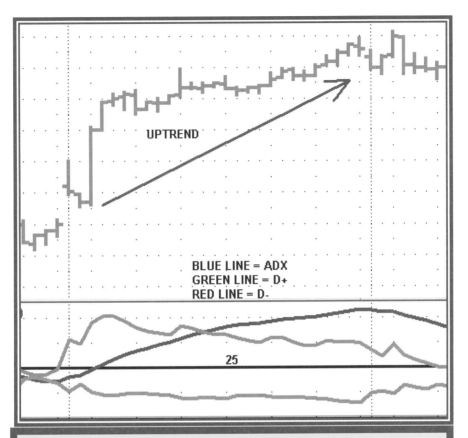

UPTREND

BLUE LINE = ADX
GREEN LINE = D+
RED LINE = D-

25

**AVERAGE DIRECTIONAL MOVEMENT INDEX—ADX
S&P E-MINI 15 MINUTE CHART**

- The E-Mini chart shows a strong uptrend. The ADX (blue line) shows a strong move because it has moved above 25 (black line). This confirms that the market is in a trend.
- The Green Line (+ DM positive directional movement) is above the Red Line (– DM negative directional movement) this is bullish and you need to buy the market. If – DM is above + DM, this is a bearish scenario and the market needs to be sold.
- This chart shows one of the best buy signals because +DM and ADX are both above the – DM and the ADX line is increasing.

Figure 68

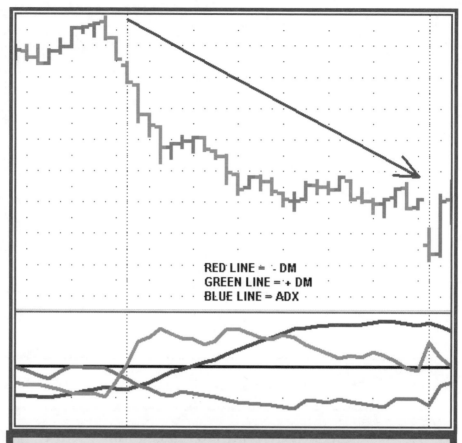

RED LINE = – DM
GREEN LINE = + DM
BLUE LINE = ADX

AVERAGE DIRECTIONAL MOVEMENT INDEX—ADX
S&P E-MINI 15 MINUTE CHART

- The E-Mini chart shows a strong downtrend. The ADX rises to a value greater than 25, which confirms the trend.
- Since – DM is above + DM, this is bearish.
- This chart shows one of the best sell signals because the –DM line and the ADX are above +DM line and ADX is increasing.

Figure 69

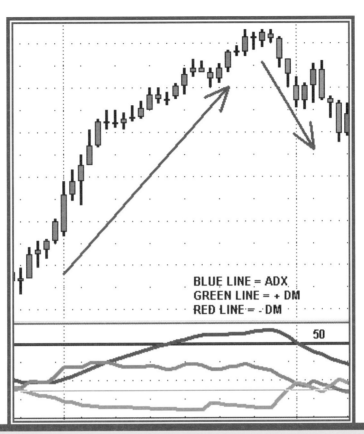

AVERAGE DIRECTIONAL MOVEMENT INDEX–ADX
S&P E-MINI 15 MINUTE CHART

- The ADX (blue line) reaches a value that is greater than 50 and becomes overbought. The ADX decreases with a downtrend in prices.
- When the ADX is greater than +DM and -DM, this indicates an overbought market.
- When ADX turns down, consider taking profits. Do not add to existing positions.

Figure 70

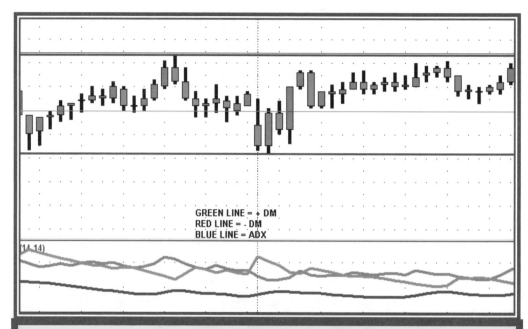

AVERAGE DIRECTIONAL MOVEMENT INDEX—ADX
S&P E-MINI 15 MINUTE CHART

- The E-Mini prices show a flat, non-trending market.
- The ADX is flat and not rising. The value is moving in a range of 12 to 14.
- When ADX is below +DM and –DM, this suggests a non-trending market.

Figure 71

MISCELLANEOUS INDICATORS

PUT-CALL RATIO

- A call is a contract that gives an investor the right but not the obligation to purchase 100 shares of a stock at a predetermined price. A put gives an investor the right but not the obligation to sell 100 shares of a stock at a predetermined price.

- When the put-call ratio is higher, investors are more bearish investors on the market. When the put-call ratio is lower, investors are more bullish investors on the market.

- The put-call ratio is a contrarian indicator. When it reaches exaggerated levels, the market usually corrects by moving in the opposite direction. At extreme levels, the put-call ratio is usually wrong because it is being driven by powerful emotion rather than good logic. The fear in a strong bear market causes people to sell, while the greed of an exuberant bull market makes investors buy like there is no tomorrow. A high put-call ratio at first glance may seem like a bearish signal, but may represent a bottom that is seen in panic selling. Likewise, a low put-call ratio reflects the over exuberance and optimism that is usually seen at market tops.

- Three types of put-call ratios are present. There is the equity options (those on individual stocks), stock index options (such as the S&P 100 and OEX options) and the total ratio which refers to the "CBOE" put-call ratio.

- The equity and CBOE put-call ratio charts will look similar, but the OEX ratio will not look the same. Institutions and professional traders use the OEX options as a hedging tool, which makes the OEX put-call ratio a less reliable signal of public sentiment.

- 10 day moving average of put-call ratio (CBOE).
  - Excessively bearish (Buy). Ratio is greater than .8
  - Excessively bullish (Sell). Ratio is less than .45

COMMITMENT OF TRADERS REPORT (COT)

One of the best sources that is available to obtain inside information on what professional traders are doing in the futures market is the Commitment of Traders Report (COT). The Commodity Futures Trading Commission (CFTC) collects the information on large speculative positions, small speculative positions, hedge positions, and professional positions from brokers and releases the compiled information to the public. The most profitable way to use the Commitment of Traders Report is to compare current positions to historical norms. If you find a situation where hedgers (smart money) and small speculators are on opposite sides of the playing field, try to trade in the direction of the smart money.

FAIR VALUE AND PROGRAM TRADING

The premium is the difference between the S&P 500 cash index (cash market) and the S&P 500 futures contract. If the premium becomes too large, program traders can profit by selling futures contracts and buying stocks. If the premium becomes too small, program traders can buy futures and sell stocks. Program trading helps to keep the values of both the futures and cash index in line. The formula for fair value for futures is:

$$FVF = (FVF) = U[1 + I\,(T/365)] - D$$
U = Value of cash index
I = Interest rate
T = Time for future contract expiration
D = Value of dividends

The basic reason for the premium or difference in the S&P cash index and the futures prices is that futures trading is less expensive than stock trading. A trader can also buy futures more quickly if important news hits the market. This is the reason that future prices can suddenly rise or fall and the cash stock index prices remain unchanged.

The question, "Is fair value important to trading?" is important to consider. The fair value number alone is not as important as the buy and sell programs that use the calculation. Watching the premium on a 5-minute chart and noting whether it is above or below fair value can be worthwhile. Many traders try to watch the premium in an attempt to hit a buy or sell level. The problem with trading this approach is that the buy and sell programs can be completed in seconds. For a trader to blindly try to trade based only upon this indicator is fraught with numerous pitfalls. The best approach is to use these levels when they complement a trading strategy.

SUMMARY OF MARKET INDICATORS

- Trend following indicators (lagging indicators)
  - <u>Moving Averages</u>—the average price of a futures contract over time. When prices rise above their moving average, it is bullish and is a good time to buy. When prices fall below their moving average, this is bearish and is a good time to sell.
  - <u>MACD</u> (Moving Average Convergence/Divergence)—a momentum and trend following indicator that identifies overbought and oversold conditions. It is an indicator that oscillates above and below the zero line
  - <u>ADX</u> (Average Directional Movement Index)—designed to measure and graphically show the strength of a trend. The ADX measures the difference between the Directional Movement plus (+DM) lines and Directional Movement minus (-DM) lines. This measures how much of the latest bar's price action falls outside of the previous bar's high and low readings.

- Momentum Indicators—measures whether a trend is accelerating or decelerating and if prices and are moving faster or slower. These indicators are called 'oscillators' because they fluctuate between extreme boundaries,
  - <u>Price Oscillators</u>—indicators that are created to pinpoint market turning points and overbought/oversold levels. They illustrate the emotional extremes of amateur traders. When price oscillators are overbought, prices are too high and ready to turn down. When price oscillators are oversold, prices are too low and ready to turn up.
  - <u>Stochastic Oscillators</u>—measures the position of the closing price for a market within a time interval. Prices tend to close at or near the extremes of their time period ranges during uptrends or downtrends.
  - <u>Relative Strength Index</u> (RSI)—measures market strength by monitoring changes in closing prices. A top is identified when the RSI reaches a peak and turns down and a bottom is identified when the RSI falls and then turns up. Usually a peak value of over 70 is a top and bottom value of under 30 is a bottom.

- Breadth (Strength and Weakness Indicators)
  - <u>Advance/Decline Line</u>—The number of advancing stock issues minus declining stock issues that offer a snapshot of market dynamics that are not revealed by price action.

- ■ TICK—the net difference between the number of stocks whose most recent trade occurred on an up tick and the number of stocks whose most recent trade occurred on a down tick. It is a most recent representation of net advancing issues.
- ■ TIKI—has the same characteristics as the TICK, except that it is calculated on the 30 Dow stocks.
- ■ 52 Week New High and New Low—can be used to assess the strength of the market trend. In a bull market, the number of stocks that are making new 52 week highs would be greater than the number of stocks making new 52 week lows. In a bear market, the number of stocks making new 52 week lows would be greater than the number of stocks making new 52 week highs.
- ■ TRIN Short Term Trading Index—An Index that quantifies the buying pressure relative to the selling pressure for the market as a whole.

- ● Miscellaneous Indicators
  - ■ Put-Call Ratio—a sentiment indicator calculated by dividing daily volume of put options by the volume of call options.
  - ■ Commitment of Traders Report (COT) Report— One of the best sources to obtain inside information on what professional traders are doing in the futures market. The Commodity Futures Trading Commission (CFTC) collects the information on large speculative positions, small speculative positions and hedge positions.

ECONOMIC NUMBERS

Economic numbers can create havoc for traders who ignore their importance. Economic numbers can send the market spiraling downward or rocketing upward on the morning that a report is released. For the trader, the hard part about economic indicators is understanding what they actually mean. Wall Street may interpret bad news as good news and good news as bad news. The key to deciphering the true meaning is knowing the economic context in which a report is released. When the market is running with the bulls, events have a greater likelihood of being interpreted as good news; whereas when the bears are in control, the odds are greater that the news will be interpreted as bad. A negative number released in a bull market will probably cause a slight pullback, but the market will more than likely continue its original trend. A negative number released in a bear market tends to rapidly increase the downward move in the market. The following are some of the key indicators followed by Wall Street.

(CPI) Consumer Price Index

The Consumer Price Index measures the average change in prices for a fixed basket of consumer goods and services. A rising CPI points to higher inflation and higher prices for everyday items. The Consumer Price Index and Producer Price Index are two of the more important inflation indicators that are followed closely by Wall Street. High inflation rates lead to higher interest rates and subsequent lower stock prices.

(PPI) Producer Price Index

The Producer Price Index measures the average change in prices charged by wholesale producers of commodities. A rising Producer Price Index indicates higher inflation rates. Higher inflation rates lead to higher interest rates and subsequent lower stock prices. The PPI, along with the CPI, are the most important indicators for inflation that are followed closely by Wall Street.

(GDP) Gross Domestic Product

Gross Domestic Product measures the production and consumption of goods and services in United States. It measures productivity growth and economic strength. A growth rate between 2% and 2.5% is considered good. A higher growth rate may suggest inflation. A lower growth rate suggests that the economy is stalling. It is a lagging indicator and is less important than the CPI and PPI as an indicator of inflation.

Employment Report

The weekly Employment Report measures the amount of people on payrolls and the unemployment rate. If you see increasing numbers of people on payrolls with rising payroll costs and decreasing unemployment, employment is better but inflationary pressure is increasing. With decreasing payroll costs and increasing unemployment, slower economic growth is suggested.

(NAPM) National Association of Purchasing Managers Report

This report represents the purchasing managers of twenty different industries. It is believed to be an indicator of future inflation. The index typically has an average value around 50. If the report value is greater than 50, this indicates a growing economy. A rise in inflation may be suggested when the numbers stay greater than 50 for an extended period of time.

(IP) Industrial Production Report

The Industrial Production Report measures output in manufacturing, mining and utility industries. This report is a good indicator of the overall state of the economy. It primary focus looks at capacity utilization or production capacity within the present economy.

Durable Goods Orders

Durable Goods Orders reflect new orders and shipments of major items in the economy. This report includes domestic products such as cars, building materials, and computer equipment. If demand (the number of orders) is greater than supply (the number of shipments), it can point to a new period of economic growth. If demand remains greater than supply with low unemployment, higher inflation could result. The demand will cause higher prices rather than increased production.

Retail Sales Report

Retail Sales is the most important report for consumer spending. A rising level in Retail Sales can lead to higher inflation. A decreasing level in Retail Sales could indicate a slowing economy. Retail Sales is subject to seasonal changes and is quite volatile.

Housing Starts

Housing Starts is a report that measures new home construction that has been started. The importance is this report is that it measures optimism in the economy. People do not build new homes unless they feel that the economy is good.

Construction Spending

Construction Spending measures spending on new building as well as improvements in residential and nonresidential buildings.

Consumer Confidence

Consumer Confidence attempts to quantify the confidence of individual households in the economy.

The most important question for traders to consider is what they should do about economic reports. The answer to this question depends upon the individual trader. Some traders roll the dice and ride through an economic report announcement, while other traders head to the sidelines. Our opinion is that we feel the 'Alice-in-Wonderland' mentality of Wall Street is too unpredictable. We never establish a large position before the release of an important economic report.

THE GREENSPAN EFFECT

Who is the most powerful man in the United States next to President George Bush? Who does not have to answer to anyone, including Congress and the voters and affects the lives of everyone? The answer to this question is ALAN GREENSPAN, the expert economist and head of the Federal Reserve Bank. Mr. Greenspan is commonly shown on television as he gets out of his limousine carrying a mysterious loose-leaf black binder.

He can operate the economy like a yo-yo and drive it up and down in rapid fashion. Greenspan's major responsibility is to keep the economy stable and gradually expanding and contracting. He can stimulate growth in the economy by increasing the money supply or keep the economy from overheating by decreasing the money supply.

The economy can be compared to our lungs in that the right amount of air is needed to expand and deflate our lunges when we are breathing. If we put to much air in our lungs, we can cause them to burst. If we put too little air in our lungs, we can cause them to collapse. Mr. Greenspan uses the money supply, which is the air that fills the economic lungs and tries to keep just the right amount flowing into and out of our economy. Therefore, investors and traders watch his every move to see how our economy will be affected.

In addition to controlling the money supply in the economy, Greenspan exerts control on the interest rates. This is the amount that banks charge people who borrow money. Raising interest rates makes it more difficult for companies and individuals to borrow money. This causes companies and individuals to be tighter with their money. There is less borrowing and expansion of plants and facilities. People quit going on spending sprees and buying luxury items. This lowers the demand for goods and helps to decrease the risk of inflation.

When interest rates are low, there is more buying. Companies are more aggressive in making long-term investments. This increases the demand for goods and services. As demand goes up, so do prices. Unfortunately, at the time of this writing, our economy, even with low interest rates, has slow growth with decreasing prices and rising unemployment. Greenspan is working hard to stabilize our economy in the present bear market.

A trader cannot ignore the Greenspan effect, which can cause the market to turn on a dime. We do not put on a trade position before a Federal Reserve announcement and always wait to see how the market will react to the news.

PREPARE FOR THE TRADING DAY
(GET READY TO RUMBLE)

The trading day is a war since there can only be one winner and one loser. A trader has to step into the ring prepared with knowledge, a trading plan, and use good cognitive judgment on each trade. An unprepared trader is at risk of a knockout in the first round.

GET

G — GET READY FOR WAR. The futures market has a winner and loser on every trade. A trader has to be like a boxer who can go the distance. Trading is a battle every day.

E — ENTRY. A stop cannot help a bad entry.

T — TACTICS. Each trading day, have a good plan and be prepared to follow it.

READY

R — RESPECT THE NEWS. Bad news can sink the best planned trade

E — EXIT. Know where your profit targets are before you enter a trade.

A — ACTION. Take action immediately when the time is right. Hesitation will cost you money.

D — DIRECTION. Don't think you are a psychic and try to pick the direction of the market. Let the market show you the direction for the day.

Y — YAHOO. Don't become overexcited with your winners and yell "Yahoo!". Remember to keep the same composure with winning and losing. Avoid having a bi-polar personality when you are trading. This means that you are up when you win and down when you lose.

TO

T — TRADERS DIARY. Keep good records of your trading to learn from your mistakes. Ask yourself, "Why did I take that trade?"

O — OFFSET YOUR TRADING with minimal losses. Let the big winners run and keep your losses to a minimum.

R U M B L E

R — RESPECT ECONOMIC INDICATORS. Don't think that you are good enough to always know how Wall Street will respond to released economic indicators. Avoid trading or reduce market exposure when an important economic number is being released.

U — UNDERSTAND THE MARKETS

M — MARRY. Don't marry yourself to a market position. If you put on a position and it does not move, get out of the trade. The longer you remain in the market, the greater risk of an adverse move.

B — BLAME SOMEONE ELSE. Remember that the buck stops with you. Don't feel the whole market is out to just get you. Take responsibility for your trades.

L — LEARN HOW TO SURVIVE IN THE MARKETS. Learn how to survive in the markets. Every trader makes mistakes. The ones that learn from their mistakes are the ones that survive.

E — ENERGIZE YOUR LIFE. Love your family and your country. It is important to have a life outside of trading.

RISK MANAGEMENT

EMOTION

Emotion is the heart attack of a trader. A trader who lets emotion control his trading is like a person who has recently had bypass surgery yet continues to smoke. It is only a matter of time before disaster will strike. Traders can get the same high that an athlete feels when he runs onto the field to win the Super Bowl. This emotional excitement is the recipe for ruin for a trader. A trader has to trade with his brain and not with his heart. A market position that is established based upon a gut feeling is like trying to walk across a patch of thin ice. It is only a matter of time before an account's trading capital withers away to nothing.

A good trader is methodical, patient, focused, and organized. He or she enters trades with precision and exits a winner or loser without hesitation. A real professional concentrates on what they do best and is not influenced by CNBC or the opinions of other traders when making their trading decisions.

CAN YOU TAKE A LOSS?

A losing trader is one who can never learn to take losses. These traders feel their hearts pounding and want to desperately hang on to a trade as it goes against them. Each tick that the trade moves against them causes chest pains as they hope for a miracle to turn the market around. When they finally decide to give up and exit the trade, the market suddenly comes roaring back. By this time, they want to jump off of a building, when they think of the money they could have made by reversing their position. Professional traders love to take new trader's money because they go the opposite direction in a trade. Amateurs typically buy when the market is at its high, only to see it fall like a rock when the professional traders sell the high. Losses have a terrible habit of becoming worse rather than better. A small loss can turn into large loss if not taken when the time is right.

A POSITIVE EDGE

A gambler has an edge in a casino when he can win more times than he loses. The gaming houses give free alcohol to players in hopes of altering a gambler's chance of winning. They also operate 24 hours-a-day knowing that a sleepless gambler is more likely to lose by making a bad decision.

In trading, the edge comes from a good system that is profitable when considering the costs of slippage and commission. The best trading system keeps trading simple. The fewer bells and whistles that are involved in a system, the more likely it will be that a system can be profitable. A good system will be successful in a bull or bear market and will work when markets change. If you have a 'keep-it-simple' system that works, don't change it.

TRADING CAPITAL SURVIVAL

The markets need new traders to enter the market and lose money to feed the trading industry. A new 'mark' enters the market and usually takes wild risks that destroy his trading capital quickly. The most important concept to understand is not risking too large a percentage of trading capital on each trade. Many 'new' traders want to get their initial losses back quickly and trade recklessly as a result. It is important to remember that the more money you lose, the harder it is to recover your losses. This point is illustrated below in percentages:

- If you lose 10%, you must gain 11% to break even.
- If you lose 20%, you must gain 25% to break even.
- If you lose 40%, you must gain 67% to break even.
- If you lose 50%, you must gain 100% to break even.

We practice a strict money management system. The most that we risk on a single trade is $200. This is our 4-point stop loss, which works out to 2% of our trading capital, if a trading account has $10,000. It would take a string of 50 consecutive losses to completely wipe out our trading capital. This number would change dramatically if we risked 10% of our capital on each trade. We would be bankrupt with 10 losses in a row and we would be required to dig a new grave in the trader's cemetery.

WHEN DO I GET OUT OF A TRADE?

Some traders believe that taking a profit on a trade is harder than bailing out of a loss. When the market moves in your favor, it is easy to start dreaming of your bank account being full of gold. Greed enters a trader's heart and he wants to let his profits run forever. This sometimes causes a trader to watch a profitable trade melt away with a sudden reversal due to bad market news. Use indicators to tell you when it is the right time to exit the market. Don't ever let yourself become emotionally attached to a trade.

SETTING STOPS TO SURVIVE

A good trader automatically sets a stop after entering a trade. The same amount of risk should be assumed on each trade. Try to time the entry into a trade that gives the best risk-to-reward ratio. Trading without a stop in place is like driving a car without a seatbelt. The majority of the time the seatbelt is not needed, but there could come a time when it would save your life. A stop helps decrease the damage when a trade goes bad. It may not work when prices gap through a stop level, but it is still the best defense to keep from losing trading capital. Stops should always be moved in the direction of the trade. We start out with a 4-point stop and then move our stop to breakeven, when the trade moves in our direction. Continue to move the stop behind the market to lock in profits until your profit target is reached.

TRADING RECORDS

The best way to learn from trading is to analyze previous trades. In our trading, we have to ask ourselves if we used our intellect or our emotions to make our decisions. Did we use our trading system and did it hold up to our expectations? Was our risk to reward decision appropriate and did we have good entry and exit strategies? What should have been done differently to make this trade more profitable? Try to save your trades on a daily basis and write down your reasons for buying or selling. Trading records are invaluable in helping you learn from the past to make your trading more profitable in the future.

FEAR OF PULLING THE TRIGGER

A lot of traders see a good trade opportunity and become paralyzed. They cannot 'pull the trigger' to enter the trade. We know a good trader who hired someone to trade his system because of his fear of getting into and out of the market. When a trader has been burned in the past and wears the scars of losing, he often lets his past mistakes dominate his decision making and tries to outguess the market. Then, he tries to change his system and trade from emotion rather than good logic. Don't let the market control you when you have a good system and have established money management rules. Take control of your trading destiny and control your emotions by your sheer will to survive.

THE CRITICAL IMPORTANCE OF ORDERS

A good trader learns quickly that he must learn to enter the right type of orders when trading E-Mini contracts. Entering the right type order is just as important as using the right scalpel for a cardiac surgeon. A price order should be used to achieve your goals in terms of timing your trades into the market. A correct order will help you avoid bad fills and slippage. In order to be a successful trader, you must be familiar with the various types of orders and the circumstances when they are best used. A trader must also know what kinds of orders to avoid.

MARKET ORDER

- An order to buy or sell as soon as possible at the best price available when the order arrives on the trading floor.
- This order will be filled at the 'bid' or 'ask' price opposite what you are trying to accomplish and will rarely be filled at your desired price.
- In a fast moving market, you will receive bad fills and lose money. This is a cost in trading called 'slippage.'
- Try to avoid market orders whenever possible. One exception to this policy is using market orders to exit a trade that is moving in your direction. This may result in positive slippage where you sell price is actually more than you expected.

LIMIT ORDER

- An order to buy or sell at a specific price. This type of order can only be filled at the stated price or better.
- Buy limit orders are placed below the current market price. The order will be filled at your price or below your specified price.
- Sell limit orders are placed above the current price. The order will be filled at your price or above your specified price.
- Do not enter a limit order too far away from the current market price. This could result in your missing a big winning trade. With a limit order, you cannot be certain that your order will be filled until a confirmation is returned to you.

STOP ORDER

- An order that becomes a market order when a particular price level is reached. These types of orders are sometimes referred to as stop-loss orders.
- A buy stop is placed above the market and is used to enter a long position or to protect a short position.
- A sell stop is placed below the market and is used to enter a short position or protect a long position.

- Good for exiting position when the market goes against you or for entering trades in the direction of market breakouts.
- In a fast market, a stop order can result in a bad fill that can cause you to lose money from slippage.

STOP LIMIT ORDER

- A type of stop order that has a limit price placed with it. A stop limit order becomes a price limit order when then stop level is triggered and the order may or may not be filled.
- This type of order decreases the chances of getting a bad fill, if it falls within certain limits that are set by you.
- Decreases the cost of slippage but increases the chance of missing fills.

MARKET-ON-CLOSE (MOC) ORDER

- This order to buy or sell at the end of the trading session at a price within the closing range of prices.
- Some traders call this order "murder-on-close" because of the occurrence of bad fills.
- This type of order is used primarily as an exiting strategy for day traders.

MARKET-IF-TOUCHED (MIT) ORDER

- An order to buy or sell 'at the market' if a specified price is touched.
- With this type of order, it is possible to get filled at any price and suffer a lot of slippage.
- A 'MIT' or 'market-if-touched' buy order is placed below the market.
- This type of order is good for trading when using support and resistance. Useful when buying near support and selling near resistance.

ORDER-CANCELS-ORDER (OCO)

- 'Order-cancels-order' allows a trader to have two working orders at the same time.
- When one of the orders is filled, the other order is automatically cancelled.

TRADING STRATEGIES

Trading the S&P 500 is like flipping a coin. We know from past observation of the market that the S&P 500 will close up for the day about 50 percent of the time and it will close down for the day about 50 percent of the time. This random type of behavior can humble even the best traders in the world. The emotions of traders in the markets can create price patterns that can cause an inexperienced trader to make ill-advised decisions. A strong move that looks like a sell signal for the public, is most likely viewed as something entirely different by the professional traders. In this section, we will review different trading strategies.

OPENING RANGE BREAKOUTS

An opening range breakout sets the tone for the rest of the trading day. Amateur traders buy and sell based upon newspaper articles, television reports, and even tips gleaned from conversations at parties. This influx of orders before the market opens often determines the opening range breakout. If the opening range is a large percentage of the normal daily range, it is likely to set both the high and low for the day. This high and low could provide the support and resistance levels for the remainder of the trading day. A narrow opening range is more likely to form a trend for the day, while a large opening range is more likely to reverse direction.

Amateur traders love to chase the excitement of a breakout trade, but professional traders love to sell the high and buy the low. Professional traders love a trading range where they can murder amateur traders who try to buy and sell false breakouts. The professionals are usually able to keep the market locked in a trading range, but occasionally a strong bull or bear market can form a breakout and a new trend.

Often, the opening and closing prices tend to be at the opposite ends of the daily range. If the market opens near the low of a wide opening range, it will usually close near the high of the opening range. This situation is a good time to look to buy E-Mini futures. If the market opens near the high of a wide opening range, it will usually close near the low of this range. This is usually a good day to sell E-Mini futures.

Blockbuster breakout moves have become scarce in this bear market. In order to survive, a trader taking the breakout trades must have a systematic approach and integrate their knowledge into each trade. Breakout moves are about a contraction in prices (low volatility) followed by price expansion (high volatility).

An opening range breakout is a trade taken above and below the opening range (high to low) by a certain number of ticks. A trader must be at his best in winning breakout trades, because the odds of success are not in his favor. The majority of the time the market will be in a trading range and will not break out to new highs or lows and will be dominated by professional traders who slaughter new traders trying to buy the highs and sell the lows. These professionals are like roaring lions waiting at the highs and lows of the market, for their next victim (Figure 71). The market only spends a few minutes of the trading day at the highs and lows. These few moments can provide periods of sheer terror when you suddenly get a reversal after placing your order and you watch helplessly as your position deteriorates and the market takes your stop out. During these few minutes of the day, you may feel paralyzed and unable to click your mouse to exit the trade.

Professional traders are like roaring lions that guard the highs and lows of the trading day. They love to slaughter new traders who are new meat when they buy the highs and sell the lows of a trading range. A trader soon learns that breakout trades are not slam-dunks.

Figure 72

The risk-to-reward ratio for breakouts is sometimes less than desirable. If you buy the high of the day for a breakout, your stop-loss for the trade needs to be at or below the low of the day by a certain number of ticks. The movement (volatility) of the E-Mini futures is not for the faint of heart and you may need to risk the entire range of the breakout in order for the trade to go in your favor. For this reason, a trader needs to have trading rules that will give him a better chance at success. Here are some breakout rules for survival.

Trade on inside days which is a trampoline for a jump in prices either to the upside or downside. The inside day is like a slingshot (Figure 73) that slowly stretches to maximum strength followed by a sudden release of energy accelerating price movement. Toby Crabel describes the use of the narrowest range for inside days in 4 days (IDNR4) and inside days with ranges smaller than the previous 6 days (NR7) as a good breakout tool (Figure 74). Following an inside day, the opening and closing price tend to be at the opposite extremes in price.

Crabel recommended trading these breakouts by using opening price and a preset value called 'the stretch.' The stretch value was obtained from the 10-day average of the difference between the open and the smallest value of the high and low. He would place a buy stop above the opening price plus the stretch amount and a sell stop below the opening price minus the stretch. The first stop triggered is the trade and the other stop becomes the protective stop-loss.

An inside day or NR7 creates a breakout situation that can lead to an acceleration in prices. The inside day or NR7 is just like a slingshot. It has no tension when not stretched (low volatility), but can become very powerful when stretched to its full capacity and suddenly released (high volatility). A trader needs to enter the market in this situation to have a greater chance of profits.

Figure 73

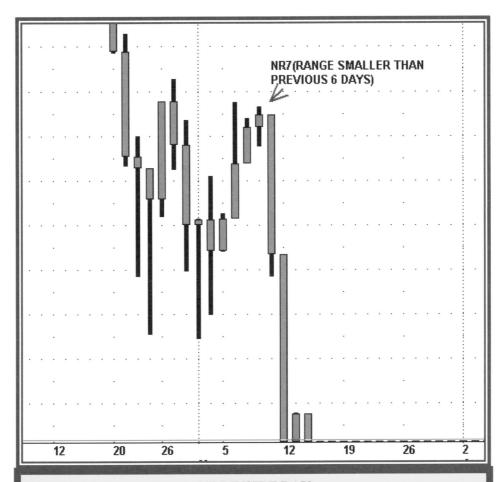

NR7 INSIDE DAY
SPX DAILY CHART

- The S&P 500 is in a downtrend and forms an area of consolidation. In this area, an NR7 or inside day with a narrower range than the previous 6 days, is formed.
- An NR7 gives a trader a greater chance of a successful breakout trade. This chart shows that the NR7 is followed by a strong downtrend.

Figure 74

- Look for gaps up (buy signals) (Figure 75) and gaps down (sell signals) (Figure 76) that occur during strongly trending days. This needs to be confirmed with candlesticks and other types of indicators, since the professionals love to keep the market in a trading range. These strong breakout days occur less than 30% of the time.

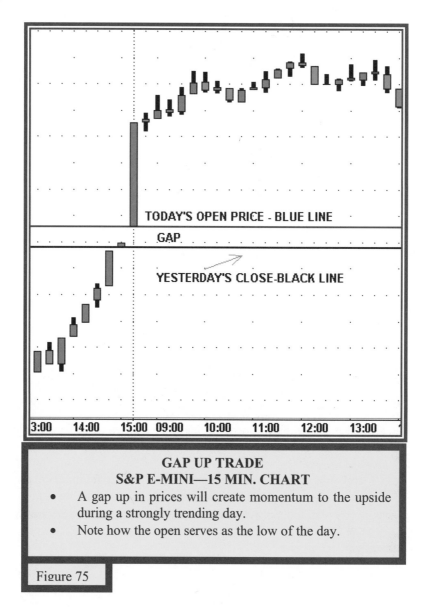

TODAY'S OPEN PRICE - BLUE LINE

GAP

YESTERDAY'S CLOSE-BLACK LINE

| 3:00 | 14:00 | 15:00 | 09:00 | 10:00 | 11:00 | 12:00 | 13:00 |

GAP UP TRADE
S&P E-MINI—15 MIN. CHART
- A gap up in prices will create momentum to the upside during a strongly trending day.
- Note how the open serves as the low of the day.

Figure 75

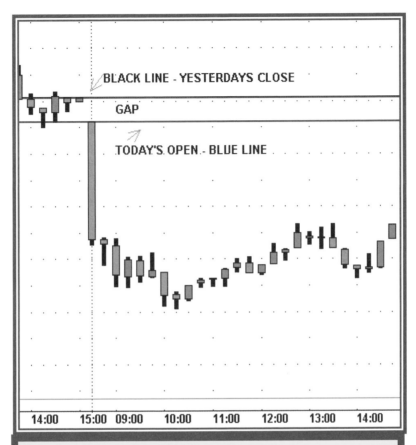

GAP DOWN TRADE
S&P E-MINI – 15 MIN. CHART
- A gap down in prices creates momentum to the downside during a strongly trending day.
- Note how the open represents the high of the day.

Figure 76

Early recognition and entry in these trades is critical for more profitable results. Remember that the early bird gets the worm. The ideal entry is in the first 10 to15 minutes where there is a greater chance of continued price movement in one direction. After more time has passed between your entry and the open, there is less chance for profits (Figure 77). The best trades will show immediate profits. The S&P E-Mini futures will usually move within 5 to 10 minutes. If there is no movement in the market, be suspicious and consider exiting the trade. If you miss the initial move, try to enter the market on a retracement.

Time is the enemy of a trader. A good trade will move quickly in your direction. If a trade is not moving, head for the exit. The longer you are in the market, the greater the chances of an adverse move.

Figure 77

Toby Crabel describes two types of early entries.

CRABEL TYPE 1 EARLY ENTRY

The first 5-minute bar has a larger range than the previous 10-days 5-minute bars. The first 5-minute bar opens and closes at the extreme of the bar (Figure 78 & 79). The second 5-minute bar also shows power in the direction of the first bar.

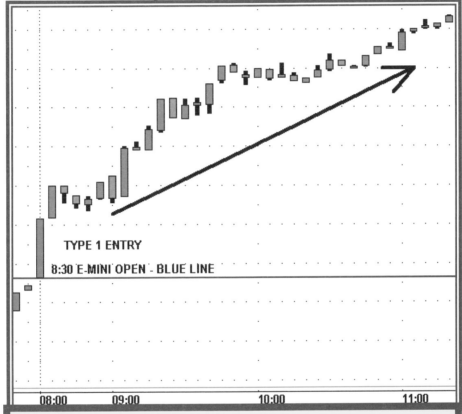

TYPE 1 ENTRY

8:30 E-MINI OPEN - BLUE LINE

CRABEL TYPE I EARLY ENTRY S&P E-MINI 5 MINUTE CHART
- The first 5-minute bar has a range that is greater than the average range of the last 10 trading days.
- The opening and closing of the first 5-minute bar is at the extremes of the price range.
- The second 5-minute bar also shows good strength in the trend direction.
- Subsequent bars in the uptrend should be of equal size or smaller. If you see bars that are larger than the first 5 minutes, this suggests that a reversal may occur.
- This chart shows a nice uptrend in the E-Mini futures. The first 5-minute bar is the largest bar in the trend. The other bars were smaller and showed a smooth trend upward.

Figure 78

139

8:30 MARKET OPEN - BLUE LINE

FIRST 5 MINUTE BAR

08:00   09:00   10:00   11:00   12

CRABEL TYPE 1 ENTRY
S&P E-MINI 5 MINUTE CHART

- The first 5-minute bar is larger than the average bar range over the last 10 days. The subsequent bars continue in a strong trend downward and are smaller than the first 5-minute bar.
- The first 5-minute bar opens and closes at the extreme of the bar.

Figure 79

CRABEL TYPE 2 EARLY ENTRY

The first 5-minute bar has a larger range than the previous 20-days 5-minute bars. The second bar shows a move in the direction of the first 5-minute bar, but it may take a period of consolidation before the move occurs. The Type 2 early entry is the same as the Type 1, except for the larger range bar over the last 20 days.

- If no Type 1 or Type 2 criteria are present in first 5-10 minutes avoid taking the breakout trade and cancel orders.
- If you entered on early entry criteria, use pullbacks to enter the market for additional positions.
- An open above the previous day's high or below the previous day's low gives a greater chance of a breakout trade. However, if you trade 2 ticks into yesterday's range, there is a 67% chance of continuing into yesterday's range

SIGNS OF BREAKOUT FAILURE

EVIDENCE OF RANGE EXPANSION
(Increasing momentum).

The bars in a trend should show equal expansion or decreased expansion. If you see larger bars than the previous bars, this indicates range expansion or increasing momentum and can lead to early failure (Figure 80).

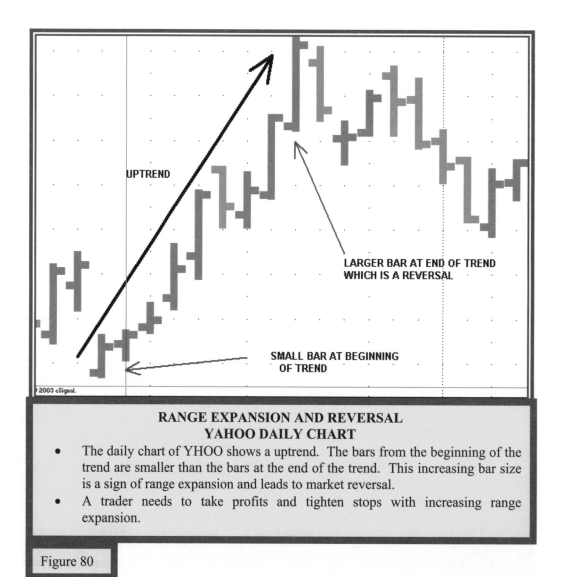

UPTREND

LARGER BAR AT END OF TREND
WHICH IS A REVERSAL

SMALL BAR AT BEGINNING
OF TREND

2003 eSignal.

RANGE EXPANSION AND REVERSAL
YAHOO DAILY CHART
- The daily chart of YHOO shows a uptrend. The bars from the beginning of the trend are smaller than the bars at the end of the trend. This increasing bar size is a sign of range expansion and leads to market reversal.
- A trader needs to take profits and tighten stops with increasing range expansion.

Figure 80

- Pullbacks or retracements should not have larger bars than the first bar. This suggests increasing momentum and early failure.
- Candlesticks can help confirm breakout failure (Figure 81).
- Take profits if you see signs of range expansions.
- A good short sale is the rapid penetration of price in the first bar by the second bar with range expansion (Figure 82).

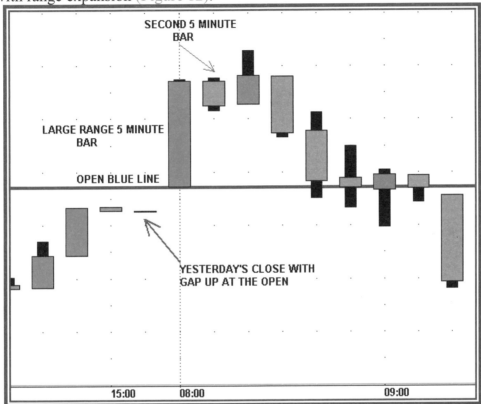

EARLY REVERSAL
S&P E-MINI 5-MINUTE CHART

- The first 5-minute bar shows a range that is greater than average for the last 10 days. There is also evidence of a gap up which usually suggests increased momentum to the upside. The first bar is opening and closing at its extreme which suggests a powerful move upward.
- The second bar does not show the continued upward price movement that is required for a Type 1 entry. This bar closed lower, suggesting a reversal. This was followed by an upward spike which is rejecting new highs and the third candlestick is consistent with a new move lower.
- This activity illustrates that 3 of the 4 criteria for Type 1 lined up perfectly, but the trade failed and was a reversal. The market always teaches us that no set of criteria is always right and that we need to be ready to reverse when the market shows us footprints of a reversal.

Figure 81

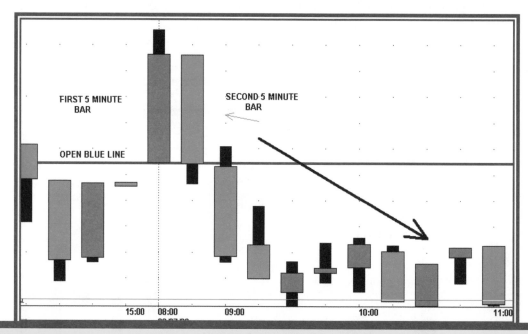

EARLY REVERSAL SHORT SALE
S&P E-MINI 5 MINUTE CHART

- The E-Mini chart shows a good uptrend in first 5-minute bar. The second bar does a countermove and the breakout trade is nullified.
- This is a good time to sell the E-Mini futures since there is a strong reversal in the other direction.

Figure 82

144

DOJI AND NARROW RANGE DAYS – TOBY CRABEL

Toby Crabel described the use of a Doji pattern and narrow range days as a way to pick reversals and trend days. He reported a 20% to 30% increase in odds in favor of the trader who used a Doji to help predict market action. Crabel described a Doji as a price bar with little difference between opening and closing prices (Figure 83) He felt that the market had indecision while it was forming a Doji and that it would mark turning points. Crabel described a narrow range day (NR7) as a day in which the range is narrower than any of the previous six days.

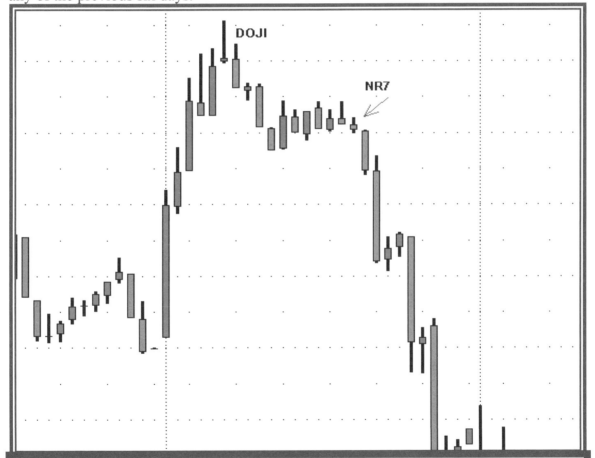

DOJI AND NR7
S&P 500 CASH INDEX 15 MINUTE CHART
- The chart shows a Doji that meets Crabel's definition of a bar with little difference between opening and closing prices. This pattern has also been called a 'shooting star' or 'upside down sledgehammer' by other authors.
- A NR7 is present followed by a strong downtrend. The presence of a Doji and NR7 lends even more strength to a change in market direction.

Figure 83   145

INSIDE DAY – TOBY CRABEL

Toby Crabel defines an inside day as one where the daily range is completely within the previous day's range (Figure 84). The inside day's high is lower than the previous day's high and the inside day's low is higher than the previous day's low. He found that an inside day was predictive of a breakout in price action and when combined with a NR4 (daily range narrower than 3 previous days) showed even more strength for a greater chance of a profitable trade.

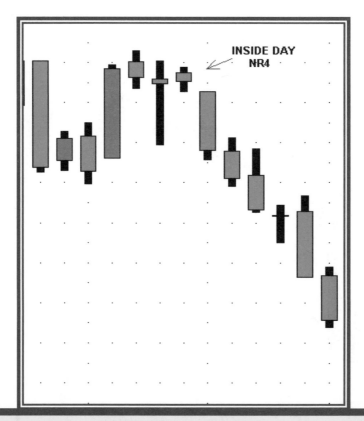

INSIDE DAY WITH NR4
S&P E-MINI DAILY CHART
- The chart shows an inside day with a NR4 resulting in a downtrend in prices. The inside day and NR4 help predict a breakout in prices.

Figure 84

Breakout trades do not occur very often in the present trading environment and the market seems to turn on a dime. The majority of the time the market will chop around between the highs and lows of yesterday. However, when a strong trend comes along, a breakout trade can become very profitable.

15 MINUTE INTRADAY BREAKOUT AT THE OPEN

Watch the first three five-minute candlestick bars in the E-Mini contract. Record the high and low of this three-bar range. Enter a buy signal when prices exceed the high of this range. Enter a sell signal when prices exceed the low of this range. Look for confirmation of the market action with candlesticks, TICK and TRIN. This trade is more effective with a gap in prices at the open (Figure 85).

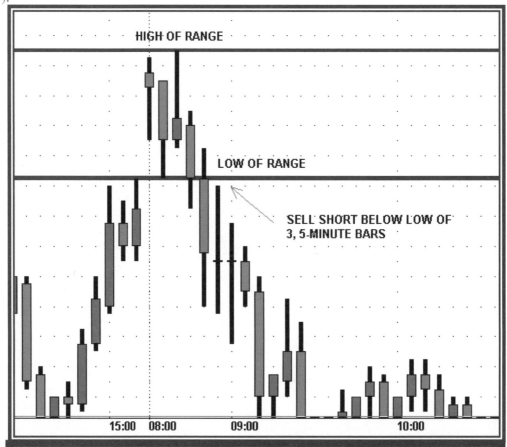

15 MINUTE BREAKOUT
S&P E-MINI 5 MINUTE CHART

- The E-Mini chart gaps up at the open. The blue lines outline the high and low of the 15 minute time period. A buy stop would be placed at the high of the range and a sell stop would be placed at the low of the range.
- The sell stop was triggered and this was a profitable trade to the downside. The protective buy stop was at the high of the day.

Figure 85

30 MINUTE INTRADAY BREAKOUT

This was the popular trade strategy during the 90's that made a great deal of money for many traders. The market was trending strongly and many traders would wait for the breakout and jump on board. Today, we have found that this breakout is difficult and frustrating to trade. The market breaks out and seems to turn on a dime.

The efficiency of the markets has caused people to enter the trade earlier and there seems to be little follow-through in the market to give a trader a chance to profit. Record the high and low prices for the 30-minute period (Figure 86). Enter a buy stop a few ticks above the high and a sell stop a few ticks below the low. This trade can make your stomach churn in agony, when you buy the high and it suddenly falls like a rock and takes out your protective stop. This is a high-risk trade in a non-trending market (Figure 87) because your stop has to be at the high or low of the trading range. A trader may have to risk 5 points to make a 2-3 points in today's market.

If you see signs of a candlestick reversal, it is better to get out of this trade in our present trading environment. However, if you see a strong trend day, this trade can be very profitable.

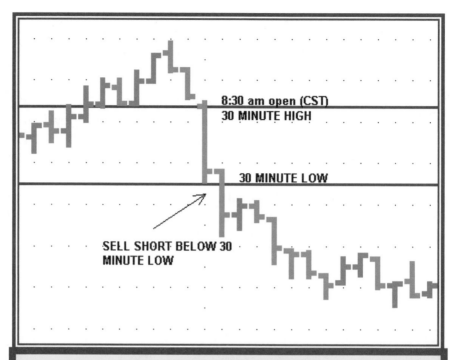

**30 MINUTE INTRADAY BREAKOUT
S&P E-MINI**

- The E-Mini chart shows a downtrend from the open. Record the high and low for the first 30 minutes of trading.
- Place a buy stop at the high of the time period and sell stop at the low.
- The sell stop was triggered and showed a profitable trade to the downside. The buy stop at the high of the day was the protective stop.

Figure 86

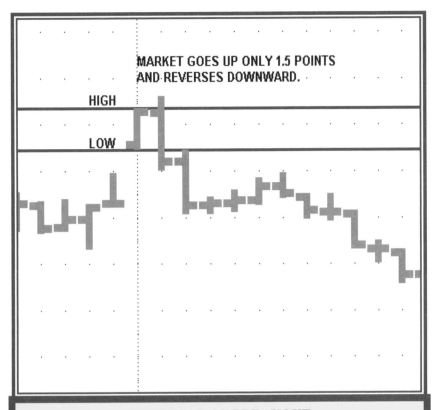

REVERSAL OF BREAKOUT
S&P E-MINI 30-MINUTE CHART

- The E-Mini chart gaps up at the open and forms a high and low for the first 30 minute green bar. A buy stop is placed at the high and sell stop is placed at the low. The buy stop is filled and the market only advances 1.5 points and reverses downward into a losing trade.

- Since there is so much uncertainty about terrorism and possible war, this is a common pattern in our present market situation with breakout trades. A breakout trade needs a trend day to have a better chance at being profitable

Figure 87

BLOCKBUSTER BREAKOUTS OF PREVIOUS DAY'S

HIGH AND LOW

We call this formation the 'Blockbuster Breakout,' because it is usually a stronger move than intraday breakouts that occur during the trading day. To clear the previous day's high and low means that the professional traders were not able to sell the highs and buy the lows forcing the market to remain in a trading range. This is strong momentum to the upside or downside and is the wave you want to ride to profits.

BLOCKBUSTER BREAKOUT SETUP

Draw a line showing the previous day's high and low on the chart. Enter a buy (Figure 88) or sell order (Figure 89) a few ticks above the high and a few ticks below the low of yesterday. Confirm the trade with price action by looking for higher highs for a buy setup and lower lows for a sell setup.

Look for candlestick confirmation and watch for any signs of reversal. Some traders use time and sales charts to confirm a long trade. If the market is going higher, there will be increased buying at the ask price which will be flashing green. If the market is going lower, there will be increased selling at the bid price, which will be flashing red.

Consider exiting the trade if the prices return into the trading range. This trade is most profitable in the first 2 hours of the trading day. On the night prior to the trade, look for inside days, NR4, and NR7 that increase the chances of a breakout on the next day.

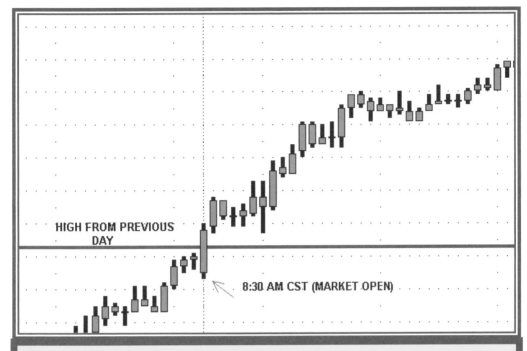

HIGH FROM PREVIOUS
DAY

8:30 AM CST (MARKET OPEN)

**UPTREND BLOCKBUSTER BREAKOUT
S&P E-MINI 5 MINUTE**

- The chart shows an uptrend in prices. This is confirmed by the candlesticks chart.
- Notice that once the prices break the previous days high, there is no retracement of prices back below the blue line.

Figure 88

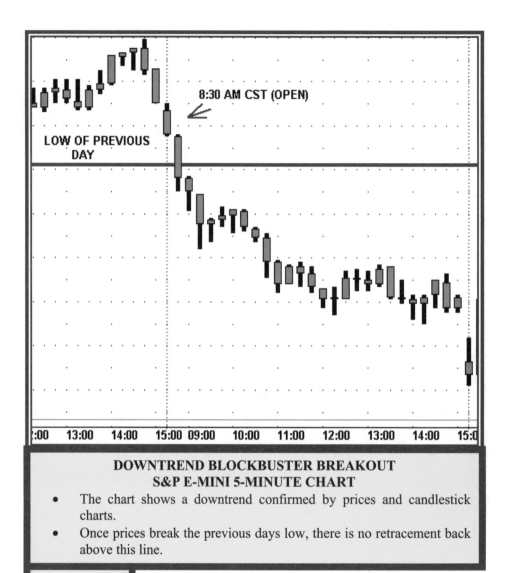

DOWNTREND BLOCKBUSTER BREAKOUT
S&P E-MINI 5-MINUTE CHART
- The chart shows a downtrend confirmed by prices and candlestick charts.
- Once prices break the previous days low, there is no retracement back above this line.

Figure 89

WILLIAMS' GAP UP "OOPS" TRADE

- This trade is designed to occur when the opening price for the day is higher than the high of the previous day. This is a rather unusual occurrence because price usually opens within the previous day's range.

- The setup for the 'gap up' trade is increased buying of E-Mini futures at the open, which drives prices above the previous day's high.

- The 'gap up' sets us up for a short sale if prices come back and penetrate the previous day's high by a certain number of price ticks (Figure 90).

- This was originally called the "Oops Trade" by Larry Williams because traders would buy and the price would suddenly lose momentum and reverse. The trader would say, "Oops, I made a mistake."

- Good news is usually the major stimulus for buying at the open.

- Gap trades are based upon day session data only and do not include the overnight GLOBEX price activity.

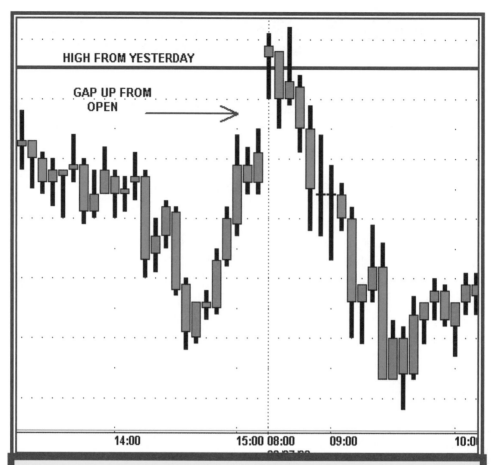

WILLIAMS' "OOPS" TRADE
S&P E-MINI 5 MINUTE CHART

- The E-Mini contract 'gaps up' at the open and exceeds the high from the previous day. This is followed by a market reversal to the downside.
- This is also called a 'gap up reversal' trade
- A trader can sell the market when the high of yesterday is broken to the downside.

Figure 90

WILLIAMS' GA P D O W N "OOPS" T R A D E

- This trade is designed to occur when the opening price of the day is lower than the low of yesterday.

- The setup for the gap down trade is increased selling of E-Mini futures at the open that drives prices below the previous day's low.

- The down gap sets us up for a buy if prices come back and penetrate the previous day's low by a certain number of price ticks (Figure 91).

- Usually bad news is the major stimulus for the selling at the open.

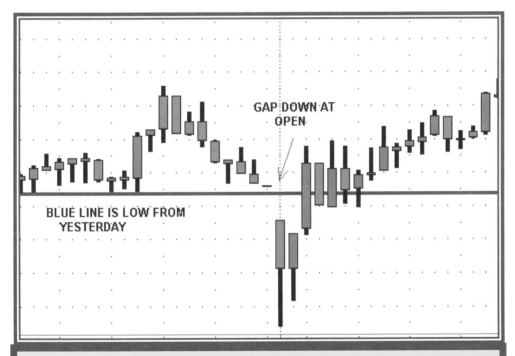

WILLIAMS "OOPS" GAP DOWN TRADE
S&P 15 MINUTE CHART

- The E-Mini chart has a 'gap down' that is lower than yesterday's low. This gap down is followed by a reversal to the upside.
- A trader can buy the market when prices have exceeded the previous days low.

Figure 91

BEAR ARCH GAP UP REVERSAL

BREAKDOWNS AT THE OPEN

The market gaps up at the open, meets resistance and falls. A trader needs to look for a pattern that looks like an arch or inverted 'U.' This pattern looks like a small replica of one of the golden arches at McDonalds. Look for bearish candlestick formations to help confirm the trade. Enter the short trade below the arch (Figure 92). The TICK and TRIN can also be confirming indicators.

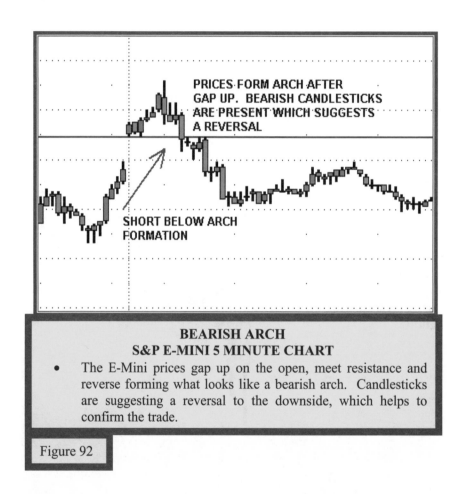

PRICES FORM ARCH AFTER GAP UP. BEARISH CANDLESTICKS ARE PRESENT WHICH SUGGESTS A REVERSAL

SHORT BELOW ARCH FORMATION

BEARISH ARCH
S&P E-MINI 5 MINUTE CHART
- The E-Mini prices gap up on the open, meet resistance and reverse forming what looks like a bearish arch. Candlesticks are suggesting a reversal to the downside, which helps to confirm the trade.

Figure 92

BULL CUP GAP DOWN REVERAL

BREAKOUTS AT THE OPEN

The market gaps down at the open, meets resistance and turns up. The pattern looks like a cup or 'U' (Figure 93). Look for bullish candlestick formations, TICK and TRIN for confirmation. Enter the trade long above the cup formation.

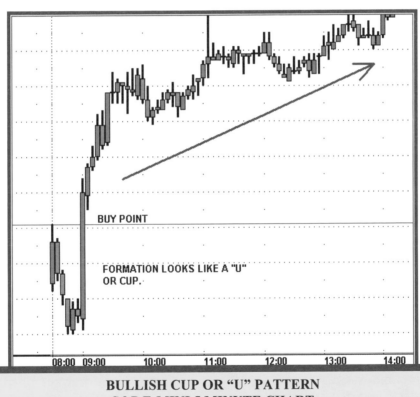

BULLISH CUP OR "U" PATTERN
S&P E-MINI 5 MINUTE CHART
- The E-Mini chart gaps down at the open and forms a 'U' pattern followed by a reversal to the upside. The buy point is a few ticks above the formation.

Figure 93

FUTURE TRADING WITH PRICE ACTION ALONE

Gary Smith is a unique futures trader who does not rely on flashing charts, moving averages, oscillators, or advance-decline lines. He trades price action alone and makes his trading decisions based upon half-hour quotes on the Dow 30, NASDAQ 100, S&P 500 and Russell 2000 cash indices. Gary has even made money while helping a friend to move across the country. During this time, his only access to the markets was calling his broker to find out data on the cash indices.

Gary has learned to focus on a few simple short-term momentum patterns that will be described below:

- ### V – Bottoms.
  A V-bottom or a spike down is good reversal tool when it occurs at the low of the day. This occurs when the Dow has been down for the majority of the day and reverses strongly to the upside and closes unchanged or mildly up for the day. Gary has found this pattern to be more effective if it occurs after a previous down day or if the Dow has been in a downtrend. The V-bottoms are less reliable on an up day or recent rising market.

- ### Late Day Surges
  The last 2 hours of trading has an acceleration of prices upward and closes at least 0.5 percent higher than the prior day's close. This resembles a V-bottom and is more effective when it occurs in downtrend or on a down day (Figure 94).

- ### 50-Minute Breakout from Open
  Gary will buy futures if the 50 minute high is exceeded between 9:20 and 11:00 a.m. CST.

- ### Extreme Gap Up or Down
  After the market gaps strongly up or down, if the market reverses, this will usually establish the trend for the day. Same as Williams "OOPS" trade.

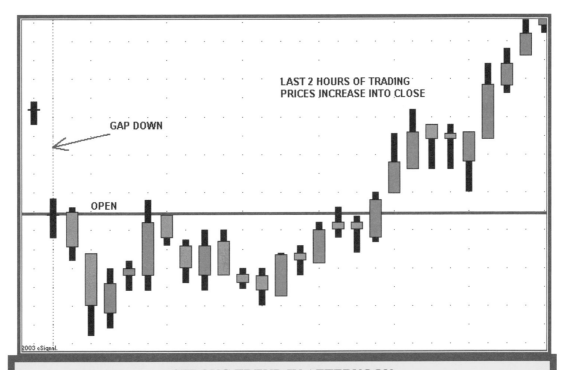

STRONG TREND IN AFTERNOON
S&P E-MINI 5 MINUTE CHART

- The E-Mini gaps down at the open and reverses, which usually establishes the trend for the day.
- In the last 2 hours of trading, the prices accelerate into the close.

Figure 94

- ## <u>Weekend Patterns</u>
  Gary feels that strength on Friday usually carries forward into Monday. He buys on the close of Friday if the Dow and NASDAQ close up 5% or more.

- ## <u>One Percent Selling Days</u>
  After a period of rising prices that lasts from 7 to 10 days, if the cash indices of the Dow 30, NASDAQ 100, S&P 500 and Russell 2000 close down more than 1%. This market activity usually indicates a change in trend. Gary gets out of his positions with a selling day, if he is long in a trade.

- ## <u>Divergences</u>
  Divergence – Look for divergence between the different cash indices to decide where to invest your money.

It is interesting that Gary Smith began trading futures in order to build up his capital to be able to trade mutual funds. His "keep it simple" approach is based upon momentum and following the strength of the market.

SWING TRADING

Swing charting is very similar to point-and-figure charting except there are no boxes and/or X's and O's. A swing is an upward or downward movement of a minimum size with no consideration of time. A swing filter determines the size of the swing that is to be described on the chart. Once prices have reversed the minimum amount, a vertical line is drawn in a column to the right of the current swing.

Swing trading is about trying to forecast the upcoming change in price movement. The idea is to have a better risk-reward ratio and place a tight stop to decrease the chance of losses. This allows a trader to minimize risk, but still have a chance to obtain good profits from a position. Swing traders are trying to take advantage of extreme price action that happens at the highs and lows of a market move. The following three patterns are good swing trades.

- Double Tops and Double Bottoms. This occurs after the market has tested a previous high or low that has been rejected. The trade will be entered in the opposite direction (Figure 95 A,B).

- Retracement in an Uptrend or Downtrend. Buy or sell when the market breaks out of an area of consolidation in a trend (Figure 96).

- Spike at a Top or Bottom with Reversal (Figure 97).

Swing trading can allow traders to compete with the professionals who love to sell the highs and buy the lows. This is a profitable strategy as long as a trend day does not occur. A trend day can fool a lot of traders because the prices seem to creep along and head steadily higher or lower. A trend day is a low volatility state that needs to be avoided with swing trading. Knowing and recognizing trend days can keep a swing trader from ending up in the trader's cemetery.

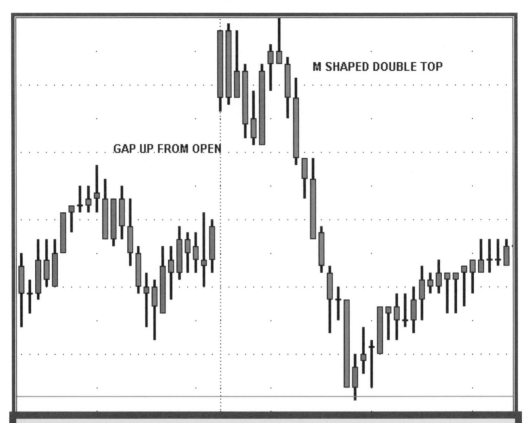

DOUBLE TOP
S&P E-MINI 5 MINUTE CHART
The E-Mini gaps up at the open and forms an 'M' shaped double top which is a low risk trade to enter to the downside. Notice how the double top was followed by a downtrend in prices.

Figure 95A

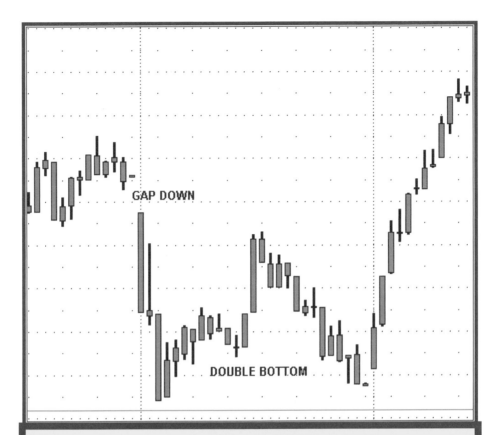

DOUBLE BOTTOM
S&P E-MINI 15 MINUTE CHART
- The E-Mini gaps down at the open and forms a 'W' shaped double bottom.
- This is a classic swing trade in buying the lows of a reversal.

Figure 95B

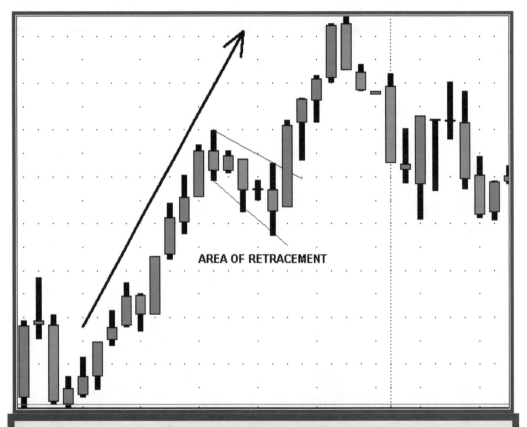

**RETRACEMENT IN UPTREND
S&P E-MINI 15 MINUTE CHART**
The E-Mini is in a strong uptrend and an area of retracement occurs. This is a good place to enter a trade with low risk. A tight stop can be placed illustrating that swing trades can be entered with low risk and still have a chance for profits.

Figure 96

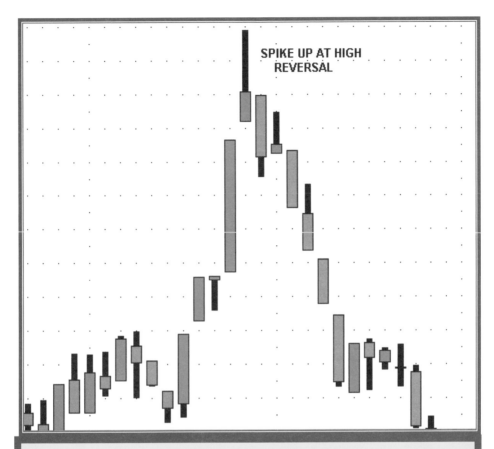

SPIKE UP AT HIGH
REVERSAL

SPIKE UP REVERSAL
S&P E-MINI 15-MINUTE CHART
- The E-Mini shows a 'spike up' which means that the market is tired and is at exhaustion point and is ready to reverse.
- This is a good swing trade to enter at the high of the day for a reversal to the downside. This is a low risk trade.

Figure 97

FIBONACCI STRATEGIES

Leonardo Pisano, who was also known as Leonardo Fibonacci, was a mathematician born in Pisa, Italy around the year 1170 A.D. He used a sequence of numbers that we know as the Fibonacci numbers to investigate the number of rabbits that would be produced in 1 year if he started with two rabbits and the rabbits reproduced once a month. The Fibonacci series is a number progression in which each successive number is the sum of the two preceding numbers. The number begins with 1 and continues as follows: 1, 2, 3, 5, 8, 13, 21, 34, 55, 89, 144, 233, 377, and so on.

$$
\begin{aligned}
1 + 1 &= 2 \\
1 + 2 &= 3 \\
2 + 3 &= 5 \\
3 + 5 &= 8 \\
5 + 8 &= 13 \\
8 + 13 &= 21 \\
21 + 13 &= 34 \\
34 + 55 &= 89 \\
55 + 89 &= 144 \\
89 + 144 &= 233 \\
144 + 233 &= 377
\end{aligned}
$$

After the first four numbers, if you divide a number in the series by the next lower number, it will settle to a particular number called the 'Golden Ratio' or 'Golden Number.' This 'Golden Number' has a value of approximately 1.61804 and is represented by the Greek letter "Phi."

$$
\begin{aligned}
377 / 233 &= 1.618025 \\
233 / 144 &= 1.61805 \\
144 / 89 &= 1.61797 \\
89 / 55 &= 1.6181818 \\
55 / 34 &= 1.617647 \\
34 / 21 &= 1.619047 \\
21 / 13 &= 1.61538 \\
13 / 8 &= 1.6250 \\
8 / 5 &= 1.60000 \\
5 / 3 &= 1.66666 \\
3 / 2 &= 1.50000 \\
2 / 1 &= 2.00000
\end{aligned}
$$

If you divide a number in the above series by a higher number, except for the first four numbers, it will settle down to .618. This is represented by "phi," which has a small "p" and represents the decimal part of 1.618. It should also be noted that the higher the numbers, the closer to .618 and 1.618 the ratios between the numbers become.

1 / 2	=	.5
2 / 3	=	.66
3 /5	=	.60
5 / 8	=	.625
8 / 13	=	.6153846
13 / 21	=	.6190476
21 / 34	=	.6176479
34/ 55	=	.6181818
89 / 144	=	.6180555
144 / 233	=	.61802575

The Fibonacci series of numbers are all about us in our universe. They were used in the famous paintings such as the Mona Lisa and the Last Supper by Leonardo da Vinci. They are present in petals of flowers, spirals of seashells, patterns of galaxies and in the Egyptian Pyramids (Figure 98). Fibonacci ratios are also used in trading to calculate price targets and retracement levels.

- Top Left – Pyramids
- Top Right – Mona Lisa
- Bottom Left – Spirals of Seashells
- Bottom Right - Galaxies

Figure 98

Example of calculating a price target.

For example:
If the E-Mini rallies from 20 to 40 and then pulls back to 30.

- Multiply the rally (40 –20 = 20) x 1.618= 32.36

- Add the pullback (30) + 32.6 = 62.6 projected price target

Example of calculating a retracement or pullback

For example
If a stock rallies from 30 to 60

- Find the distance of the stock movement = 30 (60 – 30)
  Multiply 30 x (.38, .5, .62)
  30 x .38 = 11.4
  30 x .5 = 15
  30 x .62 = 18.6

- Take high of rally (60) – (11.4, 15, 18.6) = retracement level
  60 –11.4 = 48.6
  60 – 15 = 45
  60 – 18 = 41.4

These retracement levels can be used to enter new trades in anticipation of a market reversal, or they can be used to take profits on existing trades. A trader who sold the E-Mini would look to take profits when the market approaches a Fibonacci retracement level, while a trader looking to buy the E-Mini would consider going long when there was a up turn after the retracement.

If the E-Mini has already bounced up 38% to 50% from its low, it is not a good place to be buying futures since this is a common reversal point. The same can be said for the E-Mini when there is a retreat from a high of 38% to 50%. This is not a good place to be selling the market short, because most of the move has already occurred.

When a trader sees a gap up or gap down from the previous close, he needs to take profits or tighten stops when the market retraces back to the middle point of the previous move. (Figure 99).

The duration of the price movements with Fibonacci create 'upward legs' and 'downward legs' on a chart. The first 30 minutes of the chart remind us of what we call 'Roller Coaster reversals' (Figure 100). The market can turn two or three times in the first 30 minutes of the trading day. On the days when the market shows a strong upward trend, the upward legs (buying pressure) (Figure 101, 102) will be greater than the downward legs (selling pressure). On the days when the market shows a strong downtrend, the downward legs will be greater than the upward legs. A roller coaster ride can mimic price moves on a chart. The prices seem to creep along when moving in an uptrend like a roller coaster slowly climbing up a hill; then the roller coaster rolls down the hill just like the selling fear that we saw when the Twin Towers in New York were hit by terrorists. A trader needs to compare the up hill movement to the down hill movement. This can give you an idea of whether you should be a buyer or seller later in the day. If the market shows choppy, no direction action, it is a sign to stay out of the market.

Sometimes the market does not go precisely to the predicted retracement level and ends up close to the predicted value (Figure 103). This may result in some bad trades for short-term traders. The ability of Fibonacci to predict price targets is not an exact science. A trader has to use good judgment along with other trading tools to arrive at the best decision. Fibonacci ratios can be helpful as a confirming indicator to support a trading decision and allow for better entries. This strategy can also help to tighten stops and lock in profits.

GAP UP RETRACEMENTS
S&P E-MINI 5 MINUTE CHART

The E-Mini gaps up 11 points from the previous open and retraces back to the 62% Fibonacci level. At approximately the middle of the range, a trader needs to take profits or tighten stops.

Figure 99

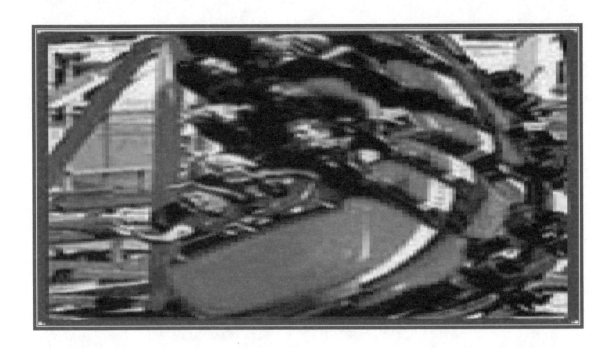

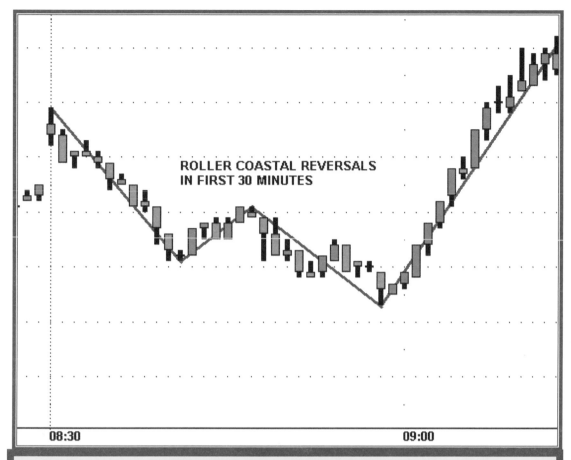

**ROLLER COASTAL REVERSALS
IN FIRST 30 MINUTES**

08:30   09:00

**ROLLER COASTER REVERSAL
S&P E-MINI 1 MINUTE CHART**
The E-Mini gaps up at the open followed by a reversal to the downside which retraces upward
and then downward before finally beginning an upward trend after 9:00 a.m.

Figure 100

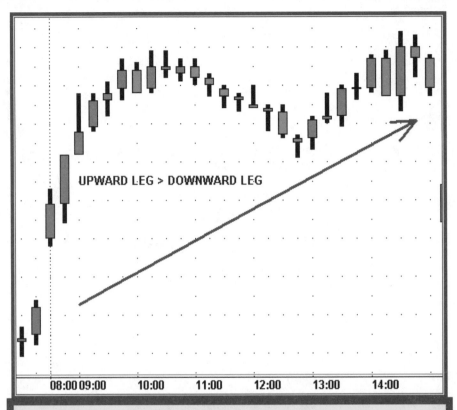

UPWARD LEG > DOWNWARD LEG

08:00 09:00   10:00   11:00   12:00   13:00   14:00

ROLLER COASTER REVERSAL
S&P E-MINI 15 MINUTE CHART
The E-Mini gaps upward with a strong trend followed by a retracement (downward leg) that is smaller than the upward leg. This is consistent with increased buying pressure.

Figure 101

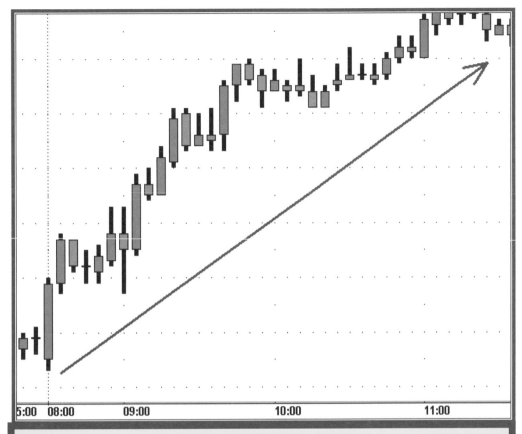

STRONG TREND AND UP LEG
S&P E-MINI 5 MINUTE CHART
The E-Mini shows a strong uptrend. This chart shows only an up leg without a down leg. This suggests strong buying pressure.

Figure 102

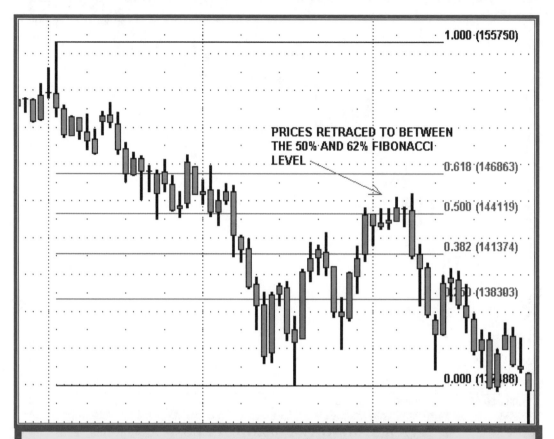

1.000 (155750)

PRICES RETRACED TO BETWEEN
THE 50% AND 62% FIBONACCI
LEVEL

0.618 (146863)

0.500 (144119)

0.382 (141374)

0.250 (138303)

0.000 (1?2?88)

S&P E-MINI AND FIBONACCI RETRACEMENTS

The E-Mini makes a high of 1530 on 9/1/2000 and then goes into a downtrend and makes a low of 1308 on 10/18/2000. Fibonacci retracement levels did not correlate exactly with the expected pullback before the continuation in the downtrend. The S&P retraced between the 50% and 62% Fibonacci levels. Fibonacci should be used with other tools and good judgment to confirm trades.

Figure 103

TOM BUSBY'S – A ROADMAP TO TRADING

Tom Busby has popularized a technique for trading E-Mini futures that consists of key numbers, time-of-day, and proprietary software called the "Roadmap" (Figure 104). Tom created the key numbers by noticing the repetition of seeing the same numbers acting as support and resistance in the market. The support area would be where buyers would take control and the resistance area would be where sellers would flex their muscles and take over. Tom created the time-of-day method based upon the assumption that he would only trade when the odds were in his favor for making money.

He felt that trading all day long would be ineffective and decrease his chances of being a successful trader. So, he created "trade zones" during the day for trading and he follows his rules for not trading outside of these time zones. Tom feels that people are creatures of habit and that their actions are reflected in the prices of the S&P Index. For example, money managers and brokers go to lunch and trading volume decreases dramatically during this time only to pick up again later in the day.

The 'Roadmap' software was designed to tell a trader if they should be buying or selling the S&P Index. The 'Roadmap' uses different indicators such as the TICK, TRIN, Morgan Stanley Tech Index, NASDAQ Composite Index, Dow Jones futures and NASDAQ futures. Each of these indicators flashes green or red. A signal to buy is presented when all of the indicators flash green; a signal to sell is when all of the indicators flash red.

Busby has divided the trading day into three trading zones:

- Trading Zone 1 - 8:30 a.m. to 9:15 a.m. (CST)
- Trading Zone 2 - 12:30 p.m. to 1:15 p.m. (CST)
- Trading Zone 3 - 2:15 p.m. to 2:45 p.m. (CST)

Tom has created a 9:00 a.m. reference trade, a 9:30 a.m. trade, a negative noon balloon, a positive noon balloon, and a 2:30 p.m. trade. His creation of time zones and time of day intraday trading is unique to his system.

8:32	-	-	-	-	-,-,-	-
9:00	839.80	288.69	1337.28	-296	1007.00,7925,1.19	113-22
9:30	839.50	290.46	1342.19	221	1012.50,7930,1.21	113-18
10:00	839.50	290.68	1343.01	226	1014.00,7930,1.28	113-22
10:30	837.00	289.28	1337.20	-27	1007.00,7900,1.65	113-24
11:00	836.30	289.28	1337.07	-57	1008.00,7895,1.74	113-20
11:30	-	-	-	-	-,-,-	-
12:00	833.50	287.66	1329.52	348	1000.50,7870,1.99	113-19
12:30	835.40	288.27	1331.65	544	1003.00,7880,1.97	113-17
13:00	833.70	287.94	1330.48	202	1003.00,7868,2.05	113-19
13:30	831.00	266.66	1324.05	-397	995.00,7848,2.21	113-25
14:00	834.50	287.10	1326.15	154	998.00,7875,2.12	113-19
14:30	834.50	287.19	1327.58	-145	1000.00,7875,1.89	113-19
15:00	831.50	286.06	1322.15	16	996.00,7850,2.08	113-19

ROADMAP OF THE MARKET – S&P 500

- This roadmap shows a Christmas tree pattern (flashing red and green colors) and is a sign to stay out of the market.
- A sell signal is when all indicators flash red
- A buy signal is when all indicators flash green.

Figure 104

The original 80-20 trade strategy was originated by Connors and Raschke. This strategy is based upon the principle that when a market closes near the extreme of its range, it has a good chance of having a midday reversal the next day. They found that when the market closed in the extreme of its range, there was an 80% to 90% chance that the market would open in the same direction the next day. However, the market would only close in that direction 50% of the time. Therefore, 50% of the time there is a good chance of a market reversal. We like to call this the 20 – 20 trade rather than the 80 – 20, since we want our signal to be a day that closes and opens in the extreme 20% of the range.

80 – 20 TRADE BUY SETUP

- YESTERDAY'S OPENING MUST BE IN THE TOP 20% OF THE RANGE AND THE CLOSE FOR THE DAY MUST BE WITHIN THE LOWER 20% OF THE RANGE (Figure 105).

- THE MARKET TODAY MUST TRADE GREATER THAN 1.5 POINTS BELOW YESTERDAY'S LOW. A BUY STOP MUST BE PLACED AT YESTERDAY'S LOW.

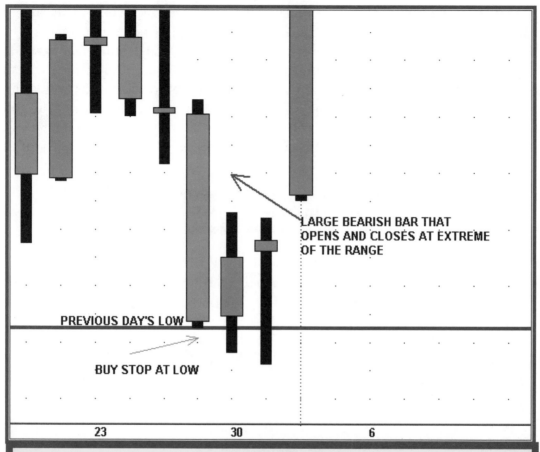

LARGE BEARISH BAR THAT OPENS AND CLOSES AT EXTREME OF THE RANGE

PREVIOUS DAY'S LOW

BUY STOP AT LOW

23   30   6

80-20 BUY SETUP
S&P E-MINI DAILY CHART

- The E-Mini chart shows a bearish daily bar opening within the top 20% of its range and closing within the bottom 20% of its range. This creates a buy setup for the next day.
- The market gaps below the previous day's low and reverses upward.
- A buy stop is placed a few ticks above the previous days low.

Figure 105

80 – 20 TRADE SELL SETUP

- YESTERDAY'S OPENING MUST BE WITHIN THE LOWER 20% OF ITS RANGE AND THE CLOSE MUST BE WITHIN THE TOP 20% OF ITS RANGE (Figure 106).

- THE MARKET TODAY MUST TRADE GREATER THAN 1.5 POINTS ABOVE YESTERDAY'S HIGH.

- A SELL STOP MUST BE PLACED AT YESTERDAY'S HIGH.

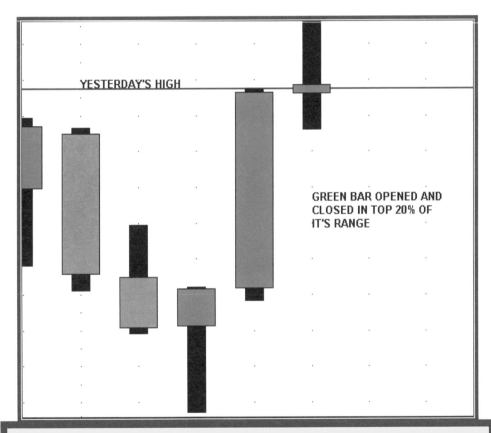

80-20 SELL SETUP
S&P E-MINI DAILY CHART
- The E-Mini shows a large green daily bar that opens and closes near the extremes of its range. The opening must be within the lower 20% of the range and the close must be within the top 20% of the range. This creates a sell setup
- The next morning the prices gap up and then reverse.
- A sell stop should be placed at yesterdays high.

Figure 106

HOLY GRAIL

The Holy Grail indicator was labeled the perfect indicator by Connors and Raschke because it was so easy to trade. This pattern is based upon using the Average Directional Index (ADX), which measures the trend strength in the market. The higher the ADX, the stronger the trend up or down.

BUY SETUP

- The 14 period ADX must be greater than 30 and rising identifying a strongly trending market.
- Look for a pullback in prices to the 20-period moving average. The ADX should decrease in value with the pullback in prices (Figure 107).
- When the price touches the 20 period moving average, put a buy stop above the high of the previous bar.
- Place a protective sell stop at the new low. If this trade is profitable, do not re-enter the market at a pullback unless the ADX turns back above 30 (Figure 108).

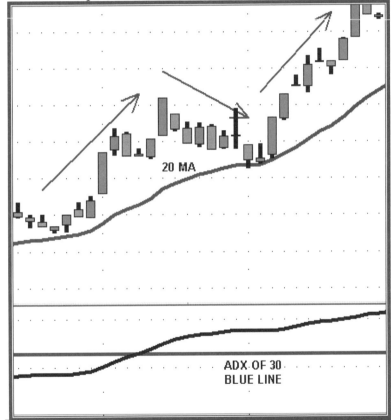

ADX AND UPTREND
S&P E-MINI 5 MIN. CHART
- The E-Mini is in an uptrend above the 20 period moving average. The ADX (black line) begins at a value of 25 and increases to above 30 (blue line).
- A buying opportunity is presented when the prices pull back to the moving average and the ADX is greater than 30.

Figure 107

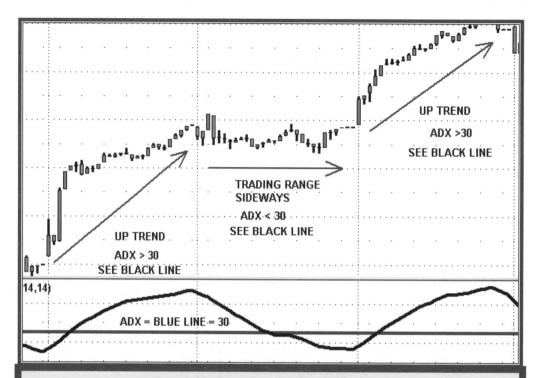

BUYING WITH ADX GREATER THAN 30
S&P E-MINI 15 MIN. CHART

- The chart shows a minute chart of 3 different days' prices. The first uptrend shows an ADX (black line) greater than 30 with rising prices. The second day show sideways movement with ADX less than 30. The final day shows a continued uptrend with the ADX greater than 30.
- This chart illustrates that it is better to wait until the ADX shows a strong trend and not reentering on a pullback in prices unless the ADX is greater than 30.

Figure 108

SELL SETUP

- The 14 period Average Directional Movement Index (ADX) must be greater than 30 and rising.

- Look for a rally in prices up to the 20-period moving average. The ADX should decrease in value with the rally in prices (Figure 109).

- When the price touches the 20-period moving average, put a sell stop below the low of the previous bar.

- Place a protective buy stop at the new highs.

- If this trade is profitable, do not re-enter the market on a rally unless the ADX turns back above 30.

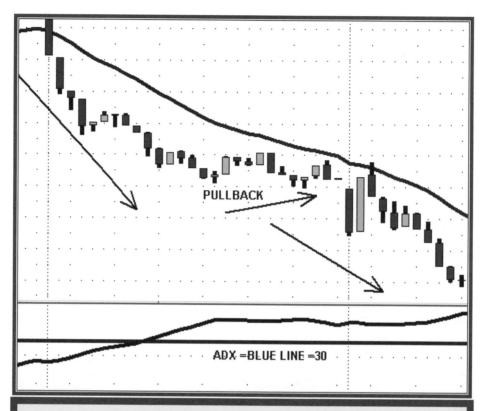

SELLING WITH ADX GREATER THAN 30
S&P E-MINI 5-MINUTE CHART

- The chart shows a downtrend in prices followed by a rally up to the 20 period moving average (blue line) with a continued downtrend in prices.
- When the rally in prices occurs, the ADX was greater than 30 (black line), which confirms a probable continuation of the downtrend.

Figure 109

The Average Directional Movement Index (ADX) measures the strength of the trend. We want to ride that wave up or down when the value of the ADX is greater than 30 (Figure 110). DM stands for directional movement. A plus (+)DM is movement up in the trend (Figure 111) and a minus (-)DM is movement down in the trend (Figure 112). The ADX is the difference between the (+) DM and the (-) DM. ADX is always a positive number with an uptrend or downtrends. It does not indicate the market direction, but suggests a strongly trending market when the value is greater than 30. A trader needs to avoid trading breakouts with a low ADX, because it can lead to capital wipeouts (Figure 113).

THE ADX REFLECTS THE STRENGTH OF THE TREND. A TRADER NEEDS TO RIDE THE ADX LIKE A WAVE UP OR DOWN. A POSITIVE DIRECTIONAL MOVEMENT VALUE (+DM) IS FOR AN UPTREND AND A NEGATIVE DIRECTIONAL MOVEMENT VALUE (-DM) IS FOR A DOWNTREND.

Figure 110

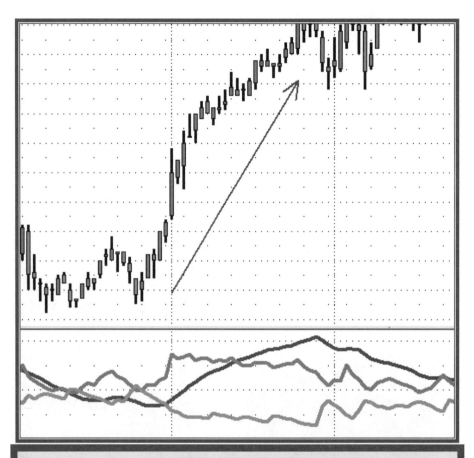

ADX, + DM AND – DM
S&P E-MINI 15 MINUTE CHART

- The prices in the E-Mini are going straight up. The blue line (ADX) is accelerating upward (> 30) and the green line is above the red line which suggests an uptrend.
- This is a strong trend day that can be profitable if you ride the wave of the ADX upward.

Figure 111

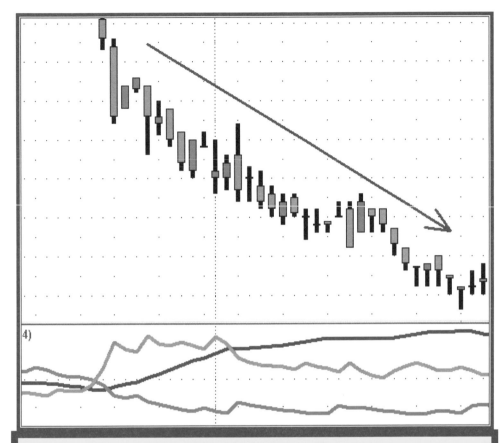

ADX, + DM AND – DM
S&P E-MINI 15 MINUTE CHART

- The E-Mini shows a strong downtrend in prices. This is confirmed by the ADX, which is greater than 30 and rising upward. Since this is a downtrend the red line (- DM) is above the green line (+ DM).
- The ADX confirms a profitable trade to the downside. The ADX is a wave every trader needs to learn to ride.

Figure 112

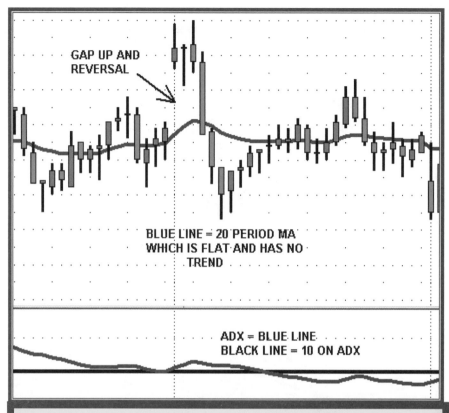

GAP UP AND
REVERSAL

BLUE LINE = 20 PERIOD MA
WHICH IS FLAT AND HAS NO
TREND

ADX = BLUE LINE
BLACK LINE = 10 ON ADX

ADX AND A FLAT MARKET
S&P E-MINI 5 MINUTE CHART

- The 20 period moving average is going sideways with the prices hovering above and below the moving average. The ADX has a value of 9 to 12 and suggests a non-trending market.
- The black arrow on the chart points to a breakout at the open which is followed by a reversal. Trying to trade breakouts in a non-trending flat market can lead to a wipeout.

Figure 113

BUY SETUP

- Today's open must gap below yesterday's low.
- The ADX must be greater than 30
- The + DM must be above the – DM.
- Place a buy stop near yesterdays low.
- Place a protective sell stop at todays low.

SELL SETUP

- Today's open must gap above yesterday's high.
- The ADX must be greater than 30.
- The – DM must be above the + DM.
- Place a sell near yesterday's high
- Place a protective buy stop at today's high.

This trade can be done without a gap up or gap down. If the ADX is above 30 and the trend is up, look for some early morning weakness and try to buy if the market recovers and moves above yesterday's close (Figure 114). The opposite can be done if the market is in a downtrend.

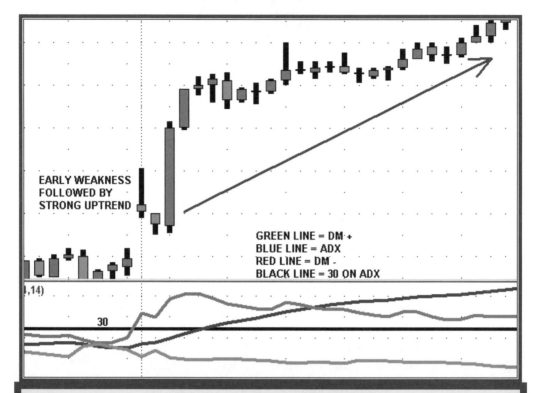

ADX AND DIRECTIONAL MOVEMENT
S&P E-MINI 15 MIN. CHART

- The chart shows some early weakness when the market opens followed by strong movement to the up side. The ADX was greater than 30 when there was market weakness and is a sign to buy if the market weakness resolves to the upside.
- The green line (+DM) is above the red line (-DM) suggesting a buy setup. If the red line is above the green line this suggests a sell setup.

Figure 114

TRENDING DAY FOLLOWED BY FLAT DAY

The markets continue to humble us even after a trend day. We have noticed numerous flat days that occur after strongly trending days (Figure 115). The present trading environment does not have much power to rocket higher and looks like the E-Minis have run out of gas after a trend day. We try to avoid trading following a big trend day due to lack of movement and choppy market conditions that cut you into pieces. Many traders give back most of their profits in the choppy markets that follow a big trend day.

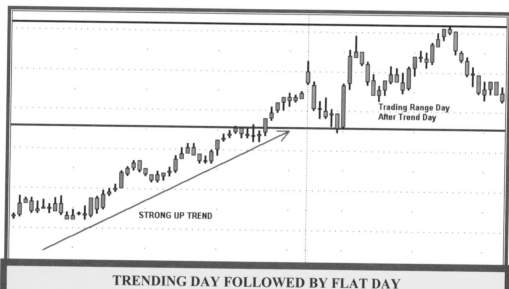

TRENDING DAY FOLLOWED BY FLAT DAY
S&P E-MINI 5-MINUTE CHART
E-Mini futures show a strongly trending day followed by a flat day stuck in a trading range. These flat, trendless days can take away profits from the previous trending day.

Figure 115

CLOSING REMARKS

This book is written for the daytrader who is in an endless struggle to understand and trade E-Mini futures. We all know that markets evolve and change and that the understanding and knowledge that is here today may be gone tomorrow. The successful trader needs to realize his limitations and continue to be a work in progress.

In this book, I wanted to review the essential elements for trading the E-Mini that would make an individual a better trader. There is no question that knowledge is essential, but I realize that the strength must come from within oneself. A trader that survives will remain humble and continue to learn. He must control his inner self, emotions and will to survive. Take this information and formulate your own trading style. You can become a good trader that will be smarter tomorrow, than he is today.

BIBLIOGRAPHY

Achelis, Steven B., *Technical Analysis from A to Z*, McGraw Hill, 2001

Angell, George, *Winning in the Futures Market. A Money-Making Guide to Trading, Hedging and Speculating*, McGraw Hill, 1997.

Busby, Tom, *RoadMap to the Markets*. Traders Press, Inc., 2002

Connors, Laurence A, Raschke, Linda B., *Street Smarts, High Probability Short Term Trading Strategies.*

Crabel, Toby, "Playing the Opening Range Breakout, Part 1," *Stocks and Commodities Magazine,* Vol. 6:9 (337-339).

Crabel, Toby, "Opening Range Breakout: Early Entry, Part 2," *Stocks and Commodities Magazine,* Vol. 6:10 (366-368).

Crabel, Toby, "Opening Range Breakout, Part 3." *Stocks and Commodities Magazine*, Vol. 6:12 (462- 465).

Crabel, Toby, "Opening Range Breakout, Part 4." *Stocks and Commodities Magazine*, Vol. 7:2 (47-49).

Crabel, Toby, "Opening Range Breakout, Part 5." *Stocks and Commodities Magazine,* Vol. 7:4 (119-120).

Crabel, Toby, "Opening Range Breakout, Part 6." *Stocks and Commodities Magazine,* Vol. 7:5 (161- 163).

Crabel, Toby, "Opening Range Breakout, Part 7." *Stocks and Commodities Magazine,* Vol. 7:6 (188-189).

Crabel, Toby, "Opening Range Breakout, Part 8." *Stocks and Commodities Magazine,* Vol. 7: 7 (208- 210).

Dobson, Edward D., *Understanding Fibonacci Numbers*, Traders Press, 1984

Lloyd Humphrey E.D., *Trading S&P Futures and Options. A Survival Manual and Study Guide*, Traders Press, 1997

Masonson, Leslie N., "Questions and Answers: Thomas L. Busby. A Roadmap to Trading," *Active Trader Magazine*, December 2001, (62- 66).

Murphy, John J., *Technical Analysis of the Futures Markets*, New York Institute of Finance, 1986

Smith, Gary, *How I Trade For A Living*, John Wiley and Sons, 2000

Sperandeo, Victor, *Trader Vic – Methods of a Wall Street Master*, John Wiley and Sons, 1993.

Wilder, J. Welles, *New Concepts In Technical Analysis*, Hunter Publishing, 1978

Williams, Larry R., *Day Trade Futures On Line*, John Wiley and Sons, 2000.

More Publications by Traders Press, Inc.®

7 Secrets Every Commodity Trader Needs to Know (Mound)
A Complete Guide to Trading Profits (Paris)
A Professional Look at S&P Day Trading (Trivette)
A Treasury of Wall Street Wisdom (Editors: Schultz & Coslow)
Ask Mr. EasyLanguage (Tennis)
Beginner's Guide to Computer Assisted Trading (Alexander)
Channels and Cycles: A Tribute to J.M. Hurst (Millard)
Chart Reading for Professional Traders (Jenkins)
Commodity Spreads: Analysis, Selection and Trading Techniques (Smith)
Comparison of Twelve Technical Trading Systems (Lukac, Brorsen, & Irwin)
Complete Stock Market Trading and Forecasting Course (Jenkins)
Cyclic Analysis (J.M. Hurst)
Dynamic Trading (Miner)
Exceptional Trading: The Mind Game (Roosevelt)
Fibonacci Ratios with Pattern Recognition (Pesavento)
Futures Spread Trading: The Complete Guide (Smith)
Geometry of Markets (Gilmore)
Geometry of Stock Market Profits (Jenkins)
Harmonic Vibrations (Pesavento)
How to Trade in Stocks (Livermore & Smitten)
Hurst Cycles Course (J.M. Hurst)
Investing by the Stars (Weingarten)
It's Your Option (Zelkin)
Magic of Moving Averages (Lowry)
Market Rap: The Odyssey of a Still-Struggling Commodity Trader (Collins)
Overcoming 7 Deadly Sins of Trading (Roosevelt)
Planetary Harmonics of Speculative Markets (Pesavento)
Point & Figure Charting (Aby)
Point & Figure Charting: Commodity and Stock Trading Techniques (Zieg)
Private Thoughts From a Trader's Diary (Pesavento & MacKay)
Profitable Patterns for Stock Trading (Pesavento)
RoadMap to the Markets (Busby)
Short-Term Trading with Price Patterns (Harris)
Single Stock Futures: The Complete Guide (Greenberg)
Stock Patterns for Day Trading (2 volumes) (Rudd)
Stock Trading Techniques Based on Price Patterns (Harris)
Technically Speaking (Wilkinson)
Technical Trading Systems for Commodities and Stocks (Patel)
The Amazing Life of Jesse Livermore: World's Greatest Stock Trader (Smitten)
The Handbook of Global Securities Operations (O'Connell & Steiniger)
The Opening Price Principle: The Best Kept Secret on Wall Street (Pesavento & MacKay)
The Professional Commodity Trader (Kroll)
The Taylor Trading Technique (Taylor)
*The Trading Rule That Can Make You Rich** (Dobson)
Top Traders Under Fire (Collins)
Trading Secrets of the Inner Circle (Goodwin)
Trading S&P Futures and Options (Lloyd)
Twelve Habitudes of Highly Successful Traders (Roosevelt)
Understanding Bollinger Bands (Dobson)
Understanding E-Minis: Trading to Win (Williams)
Understanding Fibonacci Numbers (Dobson)
Viewpoints of a Commodity Trader (Longstreet)
Winning Edge 4 (Toghraie)
Winning Market Systems (Appel)

Please contact Traders Press to receive our current catalog describing these and many other books and gifts of interest to investors and traders.
800-927-8222 ~ 864-298-0222 ~ fax 864-298-0221
http://www.traderspress.com ~ e-mail ~ customerservice@traderspress.com